What re
about this book . . .

Intimacy with and deep knowledge of the Holy Spirit are lacking in my life and many Christians. In *The Transformed Life in the Spirit*, I am encouraged and given a "toolkit" to aid in opening my heart to a deeper relationship with Jesus through the Spirit. I am excited to begin this new chapter in my faith story!

~ Pam Tolson

One of Lance's statements in the Introduction, "Our tendency toward independence and a lack of transformation can end and it will end . . .", assumes a big "if." That "if" involves both our permission, consent and participation, and the work that can only be performed by the person of the Holy Spirit. Lance defines a pathway in this book that we all can follow that will permission the Holy Spirit to do all that Jesus said he would do in John 14 and 16. Our part is to surrender ourselves each day to the Spirit and he will manage the transformation process that leads to becoming the image of Christ.

~ Harlan Goan

Our Christian brother Lance Cooper has written a very comprehensive study of the Holy Spirit. For too long, we have failed to fully acknowledge and appreciate the Spirit's constant presence in our lives! We highly recommend this book for anyone who wants a deeper awareness of the Holy Spirit's leading and equipping in their walk with Jesus.

~ Dr. Michael and Joyce Phillips

An indispensable book of awakening to "the comforter," "prayer intercessor," and "scriptural teacher" many of us incorrectly or incompletely experienced in church. Lance Cooper leads us in understanding the desire of the Holy Spirit to be moving in our lives, leading our thoughts and calling our hearts into alignment with His. Notated Scripture on nearly every page and the life experiences of his and several contemporaries' encounters with the Holy Spirit are woven by Lance into a read that will draw your attention like a magnet into bold prayer and a new life, if you are willing.

~ Dr. Jon S. Parham

With respect to the promises of Jesus (John 14:16), Lance helps you recognize the Holy Spirit in your life and discover how to ignite that Counselor for fruitful living! You'll find joy in the journey! *The Transformed Life in the Spirit of God* is a must-read book. Great insight into why we follow ourselves and not the Spirit. Explains our nature and how to Transform our mind by following the Spirit!

~ Mike and Denisa Cooper

Lance effectively uses Paul's letters and personal examples to show how we can allow the Holy Spirit to direct our lives. He gives a new insight concerning prophecy and prayer language. Easy to read and a good book.

~ Joan Passons

The Holy Spirit plays such an integral part in our relationship with God and Jesus. It is helpful to be reminded to pay attention, to listen and to actively pursue His guidance. Our walk with Jesus is more complete and more abundantly clear through the guidance of the Holy Spirit.

~ Micki Ritchie

I believe and am hopeful that the outpouring recently at Asbury represents the beginning of the last Great Awakening before Jesus returns. Multiplied thousands will need to be taught and discipled once they receive Christ. I believe and am praying that God will use your book and others to disciple these new converts. I believe that is why it is so timely that God prompted you to write it. As Helen Keller said, "Life is either a daring adventure or nothing." We were created to live on the edge to be risk takers under the anointing and direction of the Holy Spirit.

~ Joe Blackburn

Experiencing the Spirit changes us from depending on self to a conviction that the Spirit is indeed alive in us and capable of transforming us to a new self, depending on Him no matter what the circumstances. The book outlines the blessings we can anticipate but, to experience the wholeness of God's blessings, each of us has to step out of the old self in faith and depend on the Spirit to guide us. The proof of God's existence does not come from learning but from experiencing the Spirit actively working in ways that defy our human intelligence in real time and delivers a peace that is not of this world.

~ John Ritchie

The Transformed Life in the Spirit of God gave me the reminder that I needed that a true relationship with our Father is through His transforming Sprit. Lance does a tremendous job with this book by helping me have a clear understanding of what walking in the Spirit looks like. The daily lessons, meditations and prayers are extremely helpful in creating habits that transform bad behaviors that result from me trying to deal with life's challenges with my own feeble efforts. This book encouraged me to be more disciplined in my walk with the Spirit, so that I can enjoy the fruitful life and miracles the Spirit is willing to grant. Lance, thank you for your hard work that will bless so many people.

~ Steve Suggs

The Holy Spirit and His role in my life is something I have always struggled to understand. This is a wonderfully insightful study revealing how the Spirit can and does work in me every day if I will allow it.

As a Christian, for over 50 years, I still struggled to understand the Holy Spirit and how He works in my life. This study has given me a much greater understanding of the Holy Spirit. Who he is, how He works in my life and how I can enjoy a closer walk with Him.

~ Kym Lain

"Spiritual formation" is a buzz phrase these days. Churches are trying to hire one. They don't really know what one does but they think they need one. I grew up in a church fellowship that never talked about the Holy Spirit. Only recently has the topic been broached. This book presents the Spirit and life in the Spirit in a very refreshing yet challenging way. The book is full of stories of people like you and me. This book could be a commentary on the Holy Spirit in Scripture. Cooper makes the Bible texts come alive to give hope and meaning to our crazy, busy lives. I read this in one sitting. It is full of reflections at the end of each chapter. I look forward to working through those. This book will be most excellent for a small group study.

~ Dudley Chancey, PhD, Intergenerational Faith Center

THE TRANSFORMED LIFE
IN THE SPIRIT OF GOD

A Guide to The Spirit
we Often Ignore and
Need So Desperately

LANCE COOPER

The Transformed Life in the Spirit of God
A Guide to The Spirit We Often Ignore and Need So Desperately

Unless otherwise noted, Scripture in taken from the Holy Bible: New International Version (NIV), copyright ©1973, 1978, 1984 by International Bible Society, used by permission

ISBN: 978-0-9886139-7-3

Cover design: Steve Kuhn
Interior design: Adina Cucicov

Printed in the United States

InLight Publishing (words of clarity)

INLIGHT / PUBLISHING
WORDS OF CLARITY

To the most important woman in my life

"my bride"
Sheila

for her

love for Jesus
Spiritual insight and godly wisdom
devotion to our family
conscientious dedication toward making all things better
including the garden and the animals and the home
and herself

and for her grace-filled and wonderful love for me

Special thanks

to my friends
Joe Blackburn
Denisa Cooper
Taylor Cooper
Alan Eason
John Ritchie

for their

stories of transformation
and for allowing their testimonies
to be made public
for the benefit of others
and the glory of God

CONTENTS

INTRODUCTION

I want you to know how God will transform your life. I want you to know how He will do this with His Spirit and how your transformation will help change the lives of those around you. I want you to allow His Spirit to bring Jesus to you, deeper into your heart and to a relationship of truth and power that will help you see and experience . . .

- spiritual gifts you cannot find by yourself (love, joy, peace, patience, kindness, goodness, faithfulness, gentleness, self-control, healing, miracles and words)
- wisdom for the moments and direction of your life or the lives of others
- strength for what you need the power to face and handle
- encouragement when you're depressed and disheartened
- comfort for the sad and trying times of your life
- challenge for your transformation or for when you need to move in a different way

You *foolish Galatians*! Who has *bewitched* you? Before your very eyes Jesus Christ was clearly portrayed as crucified. I would like to learn just one thing from you: *Did you receive the Spirit by observing the law, or by believing what you heard?*

Are you so foolish? After beginning with the Spirit, are you now trying to attain your goal by *human effort?*

Have you suffered so much for nothing—if it really was for nothing? Does God give you his Spirit and work miracles among you because you observe the law, or because you believe what you heard? (Gal. 3:1–5)

All of us act foolishly at one time or another. We speak without thinking. We step out onto shaky platforms or build things (our lives) on foundations that are not strong, wise, or good. We rely on ourselves for godly living.

We form habits, bad habits and foolish habits keeping us from experiencing the full life that Jesus says He brings—a transformed life. The result, despite our belief in Jesus, is that we remain the same for years with . . .

- unrestrained and hurtful words or behaviors
- anxious and fearful lives
- anger and insecurity
- harsh and merciless attitudes
- judgmental and hypercritical reactions when we disagree
- impatient and short-tempered responses
- unreliable and dishonest, or treacherous, busy-body gossiping
- shallow identities based on cultural acceptance
- unforgiveness and bitterness
- sexual sins or hedonistic idols of wealth or knowledge

We see these things show up in our relationships with people, money, food, with various substances and in our relationships with God. We seem bewitched, broken and at war with ourselves and others, and this hurts us and it hurts those around us.

As the apostle Paul said two thousand years ago:

> So I find this law at work: When I want to do good, evil is right there with me. For in my inner being I delight in God's law; but I see another law at work in the members of my body, waging war against the law of my mind and making me *a prisoner of the law of sin at work within my members.* What a wretched man I am! (Rom. 7:23–24)

Looking back at my childhood and my immature beginning as a follower of Christ, I see that I was senseless and under some kind of spell—captivated by my own desire and need for control or recognition. I did not pray very often or look for God's leading and often found the same troubles over and over again because of my lack of wisdom and unrestrained behavior. During one of these times, I remember my bride, Sheila, saying to me, "Lance, why do you keep doing that to yourself?"

I think we need to ask ourselves some questions. Why do we keep doing that to ourselves? Are we bewitched? Are we delighting in something God does not want for us or want in our lives? Why don't we change and attain our goal with more human effort, with more self-discipline and willpower? Science says that we can, so why don't we?

The answers to these questions matter to our children and to those looking for evidence that God loves and talks to us and gives us direction and the power to live better lives. Whether we realize it or not, we need the healing and truth-revealing presence of God. We need Jesus.

Paul continues his thoughts about the war inside us with, "Who will rescue me from this body of death?" His answer, "Thanks be to God—through Jesus Christ our Lord!" And he gives another hint, "Those who live according to the sinful nature have their minds set on what that nature desires; but those who live in accordance with the Spirit have their minds set on what the Spirit desires" (Rom. 7:24–25; 8:5).

What does a transformed life in the Spirit look like? Read on. I promise that if you seek Jesus, He'll change your life as you surrender control of your life, and as you learn, maybe for the first time, how to live in the Spirit.

For centuries men and women have separated themselves from God. They have lived lives independent from Him and have suffered because of it. This is our tendency—to live as physical beings who are spiritually dead. This is the inheritance we've received from Adam and Eve.

Our tendency toward independence and a lack of transformation can end and it will end by the same power that created the world and raised Jesus from the dead. The promised new life will happen as we . . .

- surrender each second, minute, day, die to what we want, and desire the things that come from the Spirit of God by faith

- grow in grace toward ourselves and those we influence
- increase our faith through prayer and obedience
- seek and trust God in all our understanding and ways
- pray in the Spirit
- fast in the Spirit
- meditate upon what God says is true about us and our life with Him
- listen and respond to His Spirit within us
- walk with God again

As you give your life to Jesus, as you consecrate yourself to his will, as you trust in God and not in yourself, you will find life and have it to the full. This will happen because the Spirit of God will direct your path.

Part 1

A MIRACLE
WITHIN YOU

the old, cracked driveway by a house . . .

*Imagine today's typical homeowner who mows
his yard and keeps it looking well. John's driveway
is asphalt and, in the days since he purchased his
property, it has developed cracks and now weeds are
beginning to show themselves. Every day he drives
over it and misses the early signs of disrepair. Or,
even upon seeing it change in degrees, he allows it to
continue, nothing to nudge him, nothing to help him,
nothing but him, alone, with more than that to worry
about, to live with it and all the rest, as the holes grow
as big as his tires . . .*

*So, many of us go to church smiling politely, taking
on the chaos that weaves its web into our lives until
the holes are everywhere and we find that we needed
help beyond ourselves to keep us safe and strong.
And if we ask, then we see that in us He was always
there waiting . . . to seal the cracks and bring us home
safely every day.*

1

THE AMAZING GENESIS OF THE NEW LIFE IN THE SPIRIT

A baby enters the world broken and crying on March 13, 1950, born to Gene and Nola Cooper at St. Mary's Hospital in Knoxville, Tennessee. As new parents, they smile at the sounds of their son. They name him Lance.

My parents were survivors of World War II. I'm their first-born. With the threat of war removed, they were ready to give all they had to me. I'm a baby boomer and love life.

But, did I mention I was "broken" and imperfect? Yes, hidden from Nola and Gene were my hedonistic tendencies—desires to feel good and enjoy the pleasures of what life offered. I remember my dad telling the story of one Christmas. My presents were so numerous that they had to put them on the stairs that ran up to the second floor from the living room. As I worked my way through them, tearing the packages apart one by one, I got to the last present and asked, "Is that all?" Though my father swore to never give me a Christmas like that again, my life remained untethered and unmoderated into my teens and first years of marriage.

I lived with a mom who poured herself into being a real estate agent and a dad who worked hard as an engineer, always home at 5:30 p.m., and always drinking on the weekends. I missed my dad even though he was with us. I missed his presence and every day leaned into what made me feel OK—my performance, the applause of others and what I did.

When I was 16, God moved me out of my seat at church to accept Jesus as my Lord, but it wasn't until my thirties that living life on my own terms put me on my knees due to laziness and the unpaid bills threatening the loss of our home. God touched me a second time as I gave up and prayed to Him on my knees for help. In the days after, His Spirit began to lead me away from my inclination to sin. Today, I'm grateful for His Spirit and intervention in my life. I'm better. I'm thankful, and so is my family.

> "Now the earth was formless and empty, darkness was over the surface of the deep, and the Spirit of God was hovering over the waters" (Gen. 1:2).

When the Spirit of God draws a person near to God, something surprising and awe-inspiring happens—a new creation bursts forth. And although you cannot see the Spirit, you can later see the evidence of His work.

In the beginning, the world is in darkness, formless and empty. It's the Narnia of C.S. Lewis in winter and it's evil. It's a person broken and lost.

You cannot see the future. The way shrouds itself in darkness and fear surrounds you. Love is lost, prison doors close and people leave you. You find yourself in despair.

People live life in a cave of their own making and Christians, at times, allow another spirit to guide them into the same cave of weakness, fear and bad judgment. They live with the possibility of God's favor, but most of the time they experience a life separated from God.

In the 1520s, the expression "boo-hoo," which originally described laughter or loud weeping, became prevalent in our language. But from the early 1900s onward it came to mean only "weeping."

It's interesting that the Hebrew writer of the book of Genesis tells us, that in the beginning, the earth was "formless" and "empty," and that "darkness" was over the surface of the "deep." The three Hebrews words used for *formless*, *empty* and *deep* were *tohu* (to-hoo), *bohu* (bo-hoo) and *t-hom t-hom* (teh-home teh home).

As the other books of the Bible were written, these words were used again in several places and were translated as *vanity*, *confusion*, *a wilderness*, *emptiness*, *nothing and a deep abyss*. It's easy to see why Tolkien in *Lord of the Rings* gives us the character of Gollum, a wasted creature drawn into a life not worth living, always wanting, always needing his "little precious" ring.

It's a sad state to be without God and a wonderful thing to be drawn to Him. When we first see the Spirit in the story of our beginnings, we see Him hovering over the chaos that will become God's most magnificent creation; in which people, made a little lower than the angels, will have the breath of life breathed into them. Wow!

Beautiful, awe-inspiring, a divine spectacle of detail and glory—the waters, the land, the animals and people. Stunning and delightful, the playground and living spaces for humankind. Every day a walk with God.

Even today we see the remnants of His glory in the mountains, the planets and stars, the streams, the rocks, the canyons and the eagles and small chipmunks. The beauty of His art streams across the rainbows and in the rain and snow. When we stop, when we look and when we see what is all around us, even in a newborn child, we see the testimony and proof of Yahweh, the Lord of lords.

And then darkness came again. It swept over the creation and made it and people groan in frustration, and work became very hard. We separated ourselves from God. We were drawn away and Jesus wept.

Can you imagine how our Lord of perfect love felt when we rejected His one command in the garden and wanted only what pleased ourselves? More so, He watched His children, made in His image, drawn toward the abyss and the creature of darkness. And being spiritually dead and growing ever more wicked, we lived our lives in vain attempts to fill the abyss within us. The thirst for power, the greed for more and the daily selfish control of our own destiny were endless, as we worshiped our godless selves. We lived lives of confusion guided by the forces of an evil realm, the powers and principalities of death and destruction. We wandered in a wilderness of empty, cracked pleasures and lived futile lives separate from God.

We became so wicked that God removed all of us from the earth except one family, and later chose one nation from which to draw all of humankind back to Himself.

He saved them. They walked with Him. This nation dedicated itself to God.

Then, they separated from Him. They disobeyed Him and worshiped idols made of lifeless stone and impotent art. He then allowed this nation to be enslaved and punished by those ruling over them. They cried out. He saved them and brought them home. Over and over again, the people lived a cycle of sin and regret and repentance and each time, upon their return, He showed them His mercy and love.

Throughout these years the people chose kings and judges to lead them; and when they rebelled, prophets sent warnings of destruction.

The apostle Paul describes this well in his letter to the Romans:

> For since the creation of the world God's invisible qualities—his eternal power and divine nature—have been clearly seen, being understood from what has been made, so that men are without excuse.
>
> For although they knew God, they neither glorified him as God nor gave thanks to him, but their thinking became futile and their foolish hearts were darkened. Although they claimed to be wise, they became fools and exchanged the glory of the immortal God for images made to look like mortal man and birds and animals and reptiles.

Therefore God gave them over in the sinful desires of their hearts to sexual impurity for the degrading of their bodies with one another. They exchanged the truth of God for a lie, and worshiped and served created things rather than the Creator—who is forever praised. Amen.

Because of this, God gave them over to shameful lusts. Even their women exchanged natural relations for unnatural ones. In the same way the men also abandoned natural relations with women and were inflamed with lust for one another. Men committed indecent acts with other men, and received in themselves the due penalty for their perversion.

Furthermore, since they did not think it worthwhile to retain the knowledge of God, he gave them over to a depraved mind, to do what ought not to be done. They have become filled with every kind of wickedness, evil, greed and depravity. They are full of envy, murder, strife, deceit and malice. They are gossips, slanderers, God-haters, insolent, arrogant and boastful; they invent ways of doing evil; they disobey their parents; they are senseless, faithless, heartless, ruthless. Although they know God's righteous decree that those who do such things deserve death, they not only continue to do these very things but also approve of those who practice them. (Rom. 1:20–32)

As God led the chosen people of Israel from Egypt, He had them build the Tabernacle, the portable and earthly dwelling place of Yahweh. Aaron and his sons were consecrated as priests to preside over the sacrifices and offerings of atonement for their own sins and for those of the people. The rules were clear. To reach God, to keep His presence with them, the rules had to be followed.

> the cloud covered the tent of meeting, and the glory of the LORD filled the tabernacle. (Ex. 40:34)

> Fire came down from the presence of the LORD and consumed the burnt offering and fat portions on the altar. And when the people saw it, they shouted for joy and fell face down. (Lev. 9:24)

Fast forward many years and the Lord had led them to Canaan, the promised land, and in 1000 BC Solomon stood before the altar of the Lord in front of the whole assembly of Israel. He spread out his hands toward heaven and dedicated their nation to God:

> O LORD, God of Israel, there is no god like you in heaven above or on earth below—you have kept your promise to your servant David my father; with your mouth you have promised and with your hand you have fulfilled it—as it is today. (1 Kgs 8:23–24)

As another 400 years pass, Israel again separates itself from God in disobedience and worships idols. A nation (Babylon) rises in the east to take some Israelites captive. Others remain behind, living around the ruins of the city of Jerusalem. The rest of the people of Israel disperse themselves into different countries across the world, and 60–70 years later a remnant returns to rebuild the walls of Jerusalem and its temple.

Prophets like Jeremiah and Ezekiel cry out warnings that go unheeded and even so leave a glimmer of light for future generations:

> "This is the covenant I will make with the people of Israel
>   after that time," declares the LORD.
> "I will put my law in their minds
>   and write it on their hearts.
> I will be their God,
>   and they will be my people.
> "No longer will they teach their neighbor,
>   or say to one another, 'Know the Lord,'
> because they will all know me,
>   from the least of them to the greatest,
>   declares the Lord.
> For I will forgive their wickedness
>   and will remember their sins no more."
> (Jer. 31:33–34)

> I will give you a new heart and put a new spirit in you; I will remove from you your heart of stone and give you a heart of flesh. And I will put my Spirit in you and move you to follow my decrees and be careful to keep my laws. (Ezek. 36:26–27)

Another 400 years pass, and at just the right time Jesus comes to save us and return us to God:

> But when the time had fully come, God sent his Son, born of a woman, born under law, to redeem those under law, that we might receive the full rights of sons. Because you are sons, *God sent the Spirit of his Son into our hearts, the Spirit who calls out, "Abba, Father."* So you are no longer a slave, but a son; and since you are a son, God has made you also an heir. (Gal. 4:4–7)

When Jesus died on the cross, the earth shook, the rocks split and the guards were terrified. And something else happened:

> And when Jesus had cried out again in a loud voice, he gave up his spirit. At that moment the curtain of the temple was torn in two from top to bottom. The earth shook and the rocks split. (Matt. 27:50–51)

Since Adam and Eve, we've kept working to separate ourselves from God, while He's worked to bring Himself closer. We've put God in a building and have come to see Him a couple of times a week. We've looked to preachers and ministers to teach us about God, but have not exerted ourselves to find Him during the week. We've not thought of Him until we've needed Him. As Christians, we've acted as if He's been somewhere else: in heaven, in the Bible, in a certain location—anywhere but in us.

We don't talk about how He's working in our lives or the lives of our families. We say we believe in miracles, but not really. We believe in what we can see and touch and the research of our scientists.

We don't sit still and listen for Him and meditate on His words. We don't fast. We don't trust Him and we don't pray unceasingly. We act as though miracles have ceased and we're in charge of our own transformation.

We believe in science but not in the God who made the scientists. We see the trees but not the Maker. We hear the babies cry but believe it's OK to end their lives before they see their mothers. We eat in excess and take stress-relieving pills. Girls are boys and boys are girls. We rationalize the television shows we watch in the privacy of our homes and turn our heads when the unnatural and ungodly become the new "normal."

In 1962 and 1963, by a margin of 8–1 in the Supreme Court, recitation of prayer, the Bible and the Lord's Prayer were removed from schools. The country separated God from its children. Then, in 1973, in Roe v. Wade, the Supreme Court allowed us to kill our babies in the womb in all 50 states, leading to more than 60 million murders of unborn babies.

For the next 60 years, until 2020, one tragedy led to another:

- sexual freedom, drugs, pills
- pornography, child abduction
- school shootings
- hatred of men
- hatred of country
- 60 million abortions

- defeat in Vietnam
- World Trade Center 9/11 destruction
- family destruction
- marital destruction
- same-sex marriage
- multiple genders
- fatherless homes
- prisoners—230 thousand to 2.3 million in 35 years
- aids and sexually transmitted disease epidemics
- legalization of cannabis
- Boy Scout bankruptcy
- suicide rate increase
- pedophilia increase
- child abductions
- sociopathic increase
- drag-queen story hours for children
- math and science skill losses
- spiraling national debt
- opioid epidemic

For the sinful nature desires what is contrary to the Spirit, and the Spirit what is contrary to the sinful nature. They are in conflict with each other, so that you do not do what you want. (Gal. 5:17)

You, however, are controlled not by the sinful nature but by the Spirit, if the Spirit of God lives in you. And if anyone does not have the Spirit of Christ, he does not belong to Christ. (Rom. 8:9)

This Week

- As you work to draw close to the Lord, make this a week of repentance. Ask the Lord to make clear to you the sins for which you need repentance. And, just as Nehemiah did, pray a prayer of repentance for our nation.

- Please read Nehemiah 1:1–4.

- Each day withdraw to a place of solitude and pray this prayer or one of your own with a sincere heart. Lord God, please move me away from whatever quenches the Spirit within me . . . I do not want to live a life separate from you . . . please make me aware of the Spirit in Me . . . please make me delight in you . . . please increase my faith . . . please give me the desires of my heart and make them for Jesus and for what will be good in my life and the lives of others . . . please transform me into being more like Jesus . . . please lead me . . . please speak to me . . . please show me you're with me . . . I'm your child.

- Thank Him for your salvation and the assurance of your seat in the heavenly places with Christ as a saint and follower of Jesus.

And know this is true. You are a child of God and you do have love, power and a sound mind through His Spirit. Believe in the promise of Jesus:

But I tell you the truth: *It is for your good that I am going away. Unless I go away, the Counselor will not come to you; but if I go, I will send him to you.* When he comes, *he will convict the world of guilt in regard to sin and righteousness and judgment*: in regard to sin, because men do not believe in me; in regard to righteousness, because I am going to the Father, where you can see me no longer; and in regard to judgment, because the prince of this world now stands condemned. "I have much more to say to you, more than you can now bear. But when he, *the Spirit of truth, comes, he will guide you into all truth.* He will not speak on his own; he will speak only what he hears, and he will tell you what is yet to come. He will bring glory to me by taking from what is mine and making it known to you. All that belongs to the Father is mine. That is why I said *the Spirit will take from what is mine and make it known to you.* (John 16:7–15)

• • • •

See you next week as we learn about "The Indwelling of the Spirit of God."

an old and dusty clay pot with fine cracks . . .

In the back of an old barn lies a broken and cracked clay pot with a few crumbs of soil from plants long forgotten. The dust rides its contours that were in previous days shaped for other uses. A young child arrives with laughter looking with delight at rusted tools and hay lofts well used. He stumbles upon the pot and picks it up with all the gentleness and curiosity that only youth possesses. Looking around at other parts displayed, he carries the pot to where the sun's beams weave through the rafters, when to his surprise, the pot held in just the right way, finds the light within it brings its colors dancing on the walls. The child smiles. The pot once more breathes in new life from beams within. So it is for the broken lives the Spirit brings to the fullness always meant to be. Jesus came that they might have life and have it to the full (John 10:10).

2

THE INDWELLING OF THE SPIRIT OF GOD

Do miracles occur? Or, if you believe they occurred at some time in our history, do they occur now? Do they occur in your life?

The definition for miracle that I find on my Apple MacBook is, "a surprising and welcome event that is not explicable by natural or scientific laws and is therefore considered to be the work of a divine agency." The event is considered to be "highly improbable" or "extraordinary," and brings very welcome consequences.

At times we use the word in a flippant manner like this: "It's a miracle that . . ." Or, in sports, "a miraculous catch." Or, it would be a miracle if we could . . ." And, in those off-the-cuff comments, we often forget, "the divine agency" part.

We pray for miracle recoveries. We want a divine intervention in the lives of others or in our own lives. We at times seek help from something outside of ourselves. Then, many individuals, even the most distant from God, want Him to intervene and bring a miraculous change to a situation they face.

But, do you believe miracles occur—now? Do you believe that a divine agency works in your life? Do you? If so, you're a Christian. If not, you're not a Christian.

Think about it. Mary bears a child through the Holy Spirit. The lame walk. The blind see. Jesus rises from the dead. Murderous Saul turns into the apostle Paul. Lives radically change. The Spirit of the Lord fills the temple—the bodies of Christians who walk with Him and find joy and peace and self-control in the most difficult of times. When God touches you and me, we are never the same but are always in a state of spiritual transformation. Neither can you, a born-again creation of God, stay the same as before.

The First BIG Miracle After the Resurrection of Jesus

If you were standing there as one of His disciples, and saw Him hovering off the ground and then rising and disappearing above the clouds, you would believe in miracles. Of course, up to then you would also have seen the blind receive their sight and the lame walk and the dead brought back to life. But still, flying? Really—flying into the sky?

But that's not the miracle I want you to think of as the amazing one He had promised a few days before. Here's what Jesus said:

> If you love me, you will obey what I command. And *I will ask the Father, and he will give you another Counselor to be with you forever— the Spirit of truth.* The world cannot accept him,

because it neither sees him nor knows him. But you know him, for he lives with you and will be in you. I will not leave you as orphans; I will come to you. Before long, the world will not see me anymore, but you will see me. Because I live, you also will live. *On that day you will realize that I am in my Father, and you are in me, and I am in you.* Whoever has my commands and obeys them, he is the one who loves me. He who loves me will be loved by my Father, and *I too will love him and show myself to him.* (John 14:15–21)

Now I am going to him who sent me, yet none of you asks me, "Where are you going?" Because I have said these things, you are filled with grief. *But I tell you the truth: It is for your good that I am going away. Unless I go away, the Counselor will not come to you; but if I go, I will send him to you.* When he comes, He will convict the world of guilt in regard to sin and righteousness and judgment: in regard to sin, because men do not believe in me; in regard to righteousness, because I am going to the Father, where you can see me no longer; and in regard to judgment, because the prince of this world now stands condemned. I have much more to say to you, more than you can now bear. But when he, *the Spirit of truth, comes, he will guide you into all truth.* He will not speak on his own; he will speak only what he hears, and he will tell you what is yet to come. He will bring glory to me by taking from what is mine and making it known to you. All that belongs to the Father is mine. *That is why I said the Spirit will take from what is mine and make it known to you.* (John 16:5–15)

Now, *that's* a miracle—a big one! And an everyday one.

The more people are attached to this world and its logical, scientific realities and manufactured pleasures, the more those people separate themselves from the miracles of the divine and the less able they are to see, hear or understand what is spiritually discerned. They are lost.

But when, through faith, they repent and believe in Jesus and the good news—grace freely offered, salvation through faith—they receive the miraculous gift of the Holy Spirit as they leave the waters of baptism, and beginning in this way, each day is a miracle day! The Spirit leads them into truth and into a personal relationship with Jesus.

That's what a personal relationship with Jesus means—the Spirit helps us realize that Jesus is in the Father, and we are in Jesus, and Jesus is in us. How cool and miraculous and comforting and powerful is that?

With great certainty and strength, Jesus says, "I tell you the truth: It is for your good that I am going away, Unless I go away the Counselor will not come to you; but if I go, I will send him to you." (John 16:7)

What a miraculous statement. Jesus says it will not be good if He stays, because the Counselor will not come! He tells us that we'll not have someone to convict us, someone to make truth known to us when we need it and someone to bring others to belief. We'll be alone, separated from God and, since the time of Adam and Eve, failing to walk with God has ended in something bad.

How We're Marked and Sealed for That Glorious Day

Thousands of years ago, a particular design was embossed onto a piece of wax, lead or other material. When others saw it, they knew that it came from the authority who issued it. This emblem or seal was a guarantee and gave a message of authenticity and approval. A seal meant that something was promised. It also represented the source of the authority to make the guarantee.

A seal, used in various ways by kings and every-day people, had other purposes as well: to secure something and prevent it from losing what the seal confirmed. The seal joined two things together and prevented them from being pulling apart.

Seals were signs of covenantal or contractual agreements between people or between God and people. The terms agreed were meant to keep any outside party from dissolving the agreement.

We see these seals in the Old Testament, in the books that came before Christ. Tamar possesses the seal and cord and staff of her father-in-law, Judah, which confirm her story and keep her safe. (Gen. 38:25)

In His instructions for worship God commands, "Make a plate of pure gold and engrave on it as on a seal: HOLY TO THE LORD." (Ex. 30:26) This seal is placed on a turban around Aaron's head as he performs his priestly duties at the Tent of Meeting.

When God destroys the earth and its people with a flood, He establishes an everlasting covenant and a sign for its remembrance between Himself and all life on earth: "I establish my covenant with you: Never again will all life be cut off by the waters of a flood; never again will there be a flood to destroy the earth." And God continues:

This is the sign of the covenant I am making between me and you and every living creature with you, a covenant for all generations to come: I have set my rainbow in the clouds, and it will be the sign of the covenant between me and the earth. (Gen. 9:11–13)

I'm glad He made that covenant with us, but the best was yet to come!

The Sign of Circumcision, the Seal of the Righteous

Paul, as he speaks to the Romans, tells them that Abraham "received the sign of circumcision, a seal of the righteousness that he had by faith while he was still uncircumcised." And, if we look back to this time in Genesis, we read that God says:

"I will establish my covenant as an everlasting covenant between me and you and your descendants after you for the generations to come, *to be your God and the God of your descendants after you.*" . . . Then God said to Abraham, "As for you, you must keep my covenant, you and your descendants after you for the generations to come. This is my covenant with you and your descendants after you, the covenant you are to keep: Every male among you shall be circumcised. You are to undergo circumcision, and it will be the sign of the covenant between me and you. Whether born in your household or bought with your money, they must be circumcised. My covenant in your flesh is to be an everlasting covenant." (Gen. 17:7, 9–13)

The Seal and Sign of the New Covenant of Grace

Before Christ, seals and signs were concrete and visible to the outside world. The seal of circumcised flesh was a sign that a man belonged to God and that He'd be the God of his descendants. It meant the man would obey God's commands and worship only Him. He wouldn't worship idols. More importantly, he'd live as if he trusted God in faith.

The problem? Men couldn't do this. They couldn't keep themselves in step with the Lord. They separated themselves from Him, as their internal desires led them to outside pleasures. They were distant from God and could approach Him only through priests. They were given laws they couldn't keep perfectly and their decadent hearts required animal sacrifices to make themselves right with God. And, what about the women? Where was their sign—their seal—their salvation?

What does God do? What does He change? How does He find a way to walk with us like He did in the beginning?

At just the right time, Christ arrives on earth as a baby in a manger, and after thirty-three years of ministry dies for our sins and becomes the final sacrifice. The Spirit, placed in believing men and women, becomes the seal of our salvation. After that moment in time, nothing else counts for what we might do to make ourselves right with God—not circumcision, our church attendance or how much we give—nothing. Only Jesus.

We're now *ministers of a new covenant* with God that guarantees salvation through faith in Jesus (2 Cor. 3:6). Whoever believes through the Spirit is born again and becomes a new creation in Christ. We believe in Jesus and we are baptized in His name. "God sets his seal of ownership on us and puts

His Spirit in our hearts as a guarantee of what is to come." (2 Cor. 1:22).

A few hundred years before Christ, God spoke through a prophet:

> This is the covenant I will make with the house of Israel after that time, declares the Lord. I will put my laws in their minds and write them on their hearts. I will be their God, and they will be my people. (Jer. 31:33; Heb. 8:10)

"By calling this covenant 'new,' he has made the first one obsolete; and what is obsolete and aging will soon disappear" (Heb. 8:13). Today, ages later, we now know that through His Spirit neither circumcision nor uncircumcision means anything: what counts is a new creation. The waters of baptism do not save us through the removal of dirt from the body, but through the pledge of what a good conscience toward God does as we hear the Good News and believe in the resurrection of Jesus. (1 Pe. 3:21)

When anyone, man or woman, hears "the word of truth, the gospel of our salvation," after believing and entering the waters of baptism, they are "marked in him with a seal" (Eph. 1:13). That man or woman becomes a dwelling of the Holy Spirit in which God lives (Eph. 1:13). This is a miracle— God starts to live in us!

Then, with God, we begin a new life, a constantly transforming life, in a broken world, in the power of the Holy Spirit. Yes! Yes! And yes!

This Week

- Please read John 1–3, and as much of the rest of this Gospel as you can asking the Spirit to lead you and bring you wisdom. Before you read, please ask God to reveal what He wants you to see as you grow in the words He brings to you.

- Each day withdraw to a place of solitude and pray this prayer or one of your own with a sincere heart: *Lord God, please quiet my mind and the strivings within me and make me still and make me know that you're God and that you're exalted in all the earth. Quiet my soul. Accept my gratitude for the saving work of your Son. Strengthen, encourage and comfort my heart. Make me a minister of your new covenant. Show me someone to serve with the love of Jesus. Continue to remove from me my heart of stone and give me a heart of flesh. Have your Spirit move me to follow your commands so that people can see Christ in me. Thank you for the good news of Christ.*

- "You are a child of God." Praise Him. Thank Him and ask Him to work in your life through His Spirit and direct your path.

. . . .

a crowd responding to his seasoned song . . .

Someone came to town and he had "it." It was the "it" everyone wanted. He seemed to know. He seemed to be aware of me even though I was one of many in a crowd of people standing in front of him. Later, I also discovered that others thought this as well. He was simple to understand and amazing in his rapport with us—so authentic, so smart, a great singer and so seasoned from years of travel. And, we needed him. We needed the things he knew about. Deep inside we were alike—those who had gathered to hear—needs for ourselves and needs for our families. But, when we heard the song he sang, the music, while pleasant now, echoed later in a discordant twang.

That day we listened to notes in tune with the wisdom of the age and we stayed the same. We looked for him down the road the next day, for his reply, but all we saw was his friend paying us a visit, and so we hurriedly sat down with him and continued along the way that seemed right to us (Prov. 12:15).

3

WARNINGS AND GRIEVING THAT WILL STOP A MIRACLE 1

In the beginning, Adam and Eve experience freedom in the garden on the created earth. God walks with them and life is full. They are free—free from fear as they experience an intimate relationship between themselves and their heavenly Father. Life in the garden is good—very good.

When their trust in Him ends, they sin. They hide in shame and separate themselves from God. The very ground from which Adam has been created is then cursed and humankind is subjected to painful toil and both spiritual and physical death. The Lord God banishes them from their peaceful garden and drives them out into a broken world in chaos.

The God of heaven and earth chooses Israel, through whom to save the world. Paul tells us this sinful nation was kept locked up like prisoners. Until salvation by faith was revealed, a law was given to them to lead them to Christ (Gal. 3:22–24). By its rules, they were slaves to fear and to their sins. Each day they were told what sacrifices to offer and the strict set of instructions to follow in receiving God's forgiveness and favor. Bulls and goats and birds and lambs were killed for their sins as they watched the blood of these animals poured out over an altar.

The Bible tells us that at just the right time, Jesus, the Savior of the world leaves heaven and the presence of His Father. The messiah of the world is born in a manger to Mary, a virgin, through the power of the Holy Spirit. Grace and mercy and transformed lives enter our world through Jesus.

Jesus dies as the final sacrifice for the sins of the world. From that point in history, every man or woman who believes in Him is justified by faith, not by works or by obeying a law or by any human effort. Their circumcision is a circumcision of the heart, by the Spirit, and not by a written code. They are released from the law to serve in the new way of the Spirit— and not in the old way of the written code. Having canceled written codes with their regulations, Christ takes them away and nails them to a cross. Believers no longer live condemned because their sins are always forgiven by the blood of Christ (Rom. 2:29; 7:6; 8:1; Col. 2:14).

By faith in the saving promise and work of Christ's sacrifice, humankind receives the promise of the Holy Spirit to lead them into all truth, to strengthen them in the face of temptation, to encourage when doubt and fear are present, to comfort when experiencing pain, and to challenge when walking the wrong direction.

Jesus explains to His disciples that "if the Son sets you free, you will be free indeed" (John 8:36). By the grace of God, through faith, Jesus sets people free to live again no longer under a law, no longer slaves to fear, but children of God that they may have life and have it to the full in spirit and in truth.

When Christ dies, the curtain to the most holy place in the temple is torn in two. Then, after He leaves, the Spirit arrives, just as Jesus promised (and promises) to live inside each person, then and now, as God's new temple—each new creation living according to the Spirit's prompting and leading without a code or set of laws that must be kept for their salvation. With seats in heavenly places, they are saints broken but forgiven and transformed by the Spirit day by day into the likeness of Christ—by faith.

What if your child is due to be released from prison? What if for days you have looked out your window and down the road thinking about his return? What if you have visited him from time to time? How do you feel?

What if the day approaches? What if it takes great sacrifice on your part to free him, yet afterward he will be free of prison commands, fear and harsh treatment? What if he will be home but still at risk to the forces of his original temptation and sin and to returning to prison?

God knew this would happen to us and He sent a protector, a comforter and an encourager. The Spirit . . .

Have you ever been foolish? What did you do? What did you look like in those foolish moments and what were the consequences?

It's interesting to see the broad application of this word in the Bible . . . "his name is Fool, and folly goes with him" (1 Sam. 25:25).

- "Surely I have acted like a fool and erred greatly" (1 Sam. 26:21).
- Fools carry a resentment that kills (Job 5:2).
- "The fool says in his heart, 'There is no God'" (Psa. 14:1).
- Chattering fools come to ruin (Prov. 10:8).
- The mouth of a fool comes to ruin (Prov. 10:14).
- "[W]hoever spreads slander is a fool" (Prov. 10:18).
- "A fool finds pleasure in evil conduct" and not in wisdom (Prov. 10:23).
- "The way of a fool seems right to him" (Prov. 12:15).
- "A fool shows his annoyance at once" (Prov. 12:16).
- A fool is hotheaded and reckless (Prov. 14:16).
- The mouth of a fool leads to and gushes folly (Prov. 15:2).
- "A fool spurns his father's discipline" (Prov. 15:5).
- Money is no use in the hands of a fool (Prov. 17:16).
- "A fool finds no pleasure in understanding" (Prov. 18:2).
- Every fool is quick to quarrel (Prov. 20:3).
- A fool's lips are perverse (Prov. 19:1).
- A fool repeats his folly as a dog returns to his vomit (Prov. 26:11).
- "He who trusts in himself is a fool" (Prov. 28:26).
- A fool "gives full vent to his anger" and loses control (Prov. 29:11).
- "The fool folds his hands and ruins himself" (Eccl. 4:5).
- "[T]he fool lacks sense and shows everyone how stupid he is" (Eccl. 10:3).
- "[T]he fool speaks folly, his mind is busy with evil" (Is. 32:6).

Senseless, Following Their Own Spirit, Built on Sand, Futile Thinking

The Old Testament prophets exclaim to us:

Hear this, you foolish and senseless people,
   who have eyes but do not see,
   who have ears but do not hear . . .
They are all senseless and foolish;
   they are taught by worthless wooden idols

   . . .

The shepherds are senseless
   and do not inquire of the LORD;
so they do not prosper
   and all their flock is scattered . . .

This is what the Sovereign Lord says: Woe to the foolish prophets who follow their own spirit and have seen nothing! (Jer. 5:21; 10:8, 21 Ezek. 13:3)

Jesus says, "A foolish man's house is built on sand" (Matt. 7:26).

And Paul writes, "For although they knew God, they neither glorified Him as God nor gave thanks to Him, but their thinking became futile and their foolish hearts were darkened" (Rom 1:21).

The Seriousness of Using the Word "Fool"

Jesus tells us, "Anyone who says, 'You fool!' will be in danger of the fire of hell" (Matt. 5:22). To call someone a fool without careful thought and deliberation shows the condition of a person's heart. That's why anger, without cause and displayed in words, should remind someone of their need for repentance.

However, Paul uses this word to describe the Galatians, and calls them "bewitched," not just once but twice. Why?

> You foolish Galatians! Who has bewitched you? Before your very eyes Jesus Christ was clearly portrayed as crucified . . . Are you so foolish? After beginning with the Spirit, are you now trying to attain your goal by human effort? . . .
>
> He redeemed us in order that the blessing given to Abraham might come to the Gentiles through Christ Jesus, so that by faith we might receive the promise of the Spirit . . .
>
> Because you are sons, God sent the Spirit of his Son into our hearts, the Spirit who calls out, "Abba, Father." . . .
>
> But now that you know God—or rather are known by God—how is it that you are turning back to those weak and miserable principles? Do you wish to be enslaved by them all over again? You are observing special days and months and seasons and years!
>
> I fear for you, that somehow I have wasted my efforts on you . . .
>
> What has happened to all your joy? (Gal. 3:1, 3, 14; 4:6, 9–11, 15).

> Therefore do not be foolish, but understand what the Lord's will is. Do not get drunk on wine, which leads to debauchery. Instead, be filled with the Spirit. (Eph. 5:17–18)

"You foolish man, do you want evidence that faith without deeds is useless?" (Jas 2:20). Faith without deeds is useless and dead. Deeds without faith are useless as well. And apart from Jesus we can do nothing:

> Remain in me, and I will remain in you. No branch can bear fruit by itself; it must remain in the vine. Neither can you bear fruit unless you remain in me. "I am the vine; you are the branches. If a man remains in me and I in him, he will bear much fruit; apart from me you can do nothing. (John 15:4–5)

This Week

- Please read Galatians. Ask God to reveal an interpretation of this book that will help you see how to live out your faith today. Ask Him to reveal any way in which you or any church you have attended has not done this. Ask Him to reveal any way in which your life is in conflict with Paul's teaching.

- Each day withdraw to a place of solitude and pray this prayer or one of your own with a sincere heart:

Lord God, I want to abide in Jesus. I want to bear much fruit in you. I want to be ambitious in the good news of your salvation with my mouth and my behaviors. Guide me with the Spirit. Give me purpose and meaning in my daily walk with you and among the people around me. Show me my place in your kingdom work. Increase my faith in you and the Spirit of God. I love you.

• • • •

lost at two roads diverging in a wood . . .

I got lost one day while riding in my jeep through the back country. I remember the motor dying miles from where I started. Back there in the deep green lush of foliage and trees, it all looks the same as you walk in the forest, one tree the same as the next, as I did that day looking for my way home. Did I say it all looks the same? Yes, I had come to the same place. There it was. I could go right or left or straight ahead. One way was carefree—no limits that I could see. The other was firmly marked and showed even where my foot ought to be. The first one with pleasure untold later turned and veered into hell, while the second started pure and right and perfect but met the other as well. What to do? I had come to the same place. I waited—waited for Him to tell me—the one I could not see, and He said to step ahead into a road I could not see. That step, the road less traveled with trust unformed, has brought me life and love and peace and more.

4

WARNINGS AND GRIEVING THAT WILL STOP A MIRACLE 2

When a father welcomes home a son redeemed from prison, from those fearful conditions, from the ruins of a life shattered by sin and the blood and misery of others, he throws a party. He pulls away the curtain to let the light in. He celebrates His son's return with music and dancing. He gives him the best part of Himself without reservation—His very Spirit to live in him, to love him, strengthen him, comfort him and to help him grow stronger. In this way He promises to lead, walk and stay with His son, His returned child, to the very ends of the earth.

We've been reunited with our Father. Jesus has done this with His sacrifice and resurrection, and His Spirit has been deposited in our hearts as a guarantee of our inheritance until our redemption. He's set His seal of ownership on us and lives in our hearts. Wow, what a miracle!

We've been rescued from the life of unresolved sin and spiritual death we lived, separated from the God who made us. We're born again of the Spirit and a new creation in Christ Jesus.

We're no longer slaves to fear or sin, and by Him we cry, "Abba, Father" (Rom. 7:25; 8:15). Because of our love for the Father, we make ourselves slaves to Him; and though we're free and belong to no man, we also make ourselves slaves to those around us to win as many as possible. As the Spirit leads us, we do our best for the benefit of others and the glory of God.

We delight in the Ten Commandments, in obeying the rules and commands of God we find in the Bible, and we respond to His discipline by being trained by it. We follow the Spirit, who lives in us. And now, under His new covenant, we find many ways in which we may love others, worship Him and bring others to Jesus.

The Spirit leads us into acts of forgiveness, into loving behaviors toward others and helps us with the words we say and how we say them. He shows us multiple ways to be in fellowship with others and to carry out the Lord's desires for us as we impact the world for Christ. He teaches us to delight in the Lord and, when we do, He gives us the desires of our hearts (Psa. 37:4).

We would be foolish, having lived life in the Spirit, to go back to prison. We would be foolish to give in to a life without Christ. We would be foolish to elevate our intellect, our actions or our feelings over the Spirit's leading. If we did this, the apostle Paul might ask us, "Who bewitched you? How is it that you are turning back to those weak and miserable principles?" (Gal. 3:1; 4:9).

The Paradox of Freedom and the Warning of Bondage

We die to live and to have life to the full (Gal 2:20; John 10:10). We're born again as a new creation (1 Pet. 1:23; 2 Cor. 5:17; Gal. 6:15).

Is God more important than the Bible? Yes.
Is Jesus more important than the Bible? Yes.
Is the Holy Spirit more important than the Bible? Yes.

Is the Bible important? Yes.

Do we diligently study the Scriptures because we think that by them we possess eternal life? No! The Scriptures testify about Jesus. *We come to Jesus to have life. We walk in the Spirit to have life. We have the love of God in our hearts and that brings us life. We love God and that brings us life.* Do you love God? Do you love Jesus? Do you love the Spirit of God?

We know that the work of God is this: to believe in the one whom he sent to us—Jesus. This is the work God requires (John 6:29).

No one can come to Jesus unless the Father draws him (John 6:44). Has He drawn you by His love—by the death of Jesus and His resurrection? Whoever, having been drawn by the Father, believes in Jesus has streams of living water flow from within. The Spirit gives life and the flesh counts for nothing (John 6:63).

But, here's the paradox. To have streams of living water in us, to be free and free indeed, we must take the yoke of Jesus upon us through faith. We're then able to learn that He's gentle and humble in heart. And when we do this, we'll find rest for our souls. God will walk intimately with us again as His Spirit lives in us. We'll no longer be slaves to sin or to law. Adam's curse will be broken and we'll arrive at a new beginning, the genesis of our new life.

The Spirit of God again hovers in the depth of our souls and brings light into the chaos of our lives and we once again walk in an intimate relationship with God. And, while we still live in a broken world, His Spirit works to put our broken selves back together and to recreate our hearts and lives into the likeness of His Son. Wow! Amazing grace! Good news!

Still, even with this revealed truth, the pull of our genetic makeup and natural proclivities are strong. Just like Adam and Eve, we want to operate independently of God. Without His Spirit leading us, we want to decide what makes us and others right with God or right in the world. Many in Christ do this, and those without Him do as well.

Those without Christ place themselves under laws of their own making in order to feel right among people in the world. They may do the following:

- Buy certain brands because of what they state to themselves and to those around them.
- Drive particular vehicles to know that they have "arrived."
- Live in houses and areas that make them feel worthy.
- Talk badly about and laugh at those who don't fit their picture of good.
- Put their faith in money in the bank or in the stock market.

- Cry over lost football games or a bad score on the golf course.
- Find pride in the degrees they have or the work they do.
- Be prideful for the way they act and the power of their position.
- Be prideful for how they feel about recognition and reputation.
- Live life through their children's perfection and achievements.
- Choose sexual conquest on the internet or in the dark to feel important.

Paradoxically, Jesus offers freedom, and yet some Christians, who should be free, choose instead to be bound to a different set of "miserable principles":

- Going to church and serving there so they may feel superior or righteous.
- Placing God and His Spirit in a box of restricted movement and influence.
- Having more faith in a pattern of new rules and regulations than in God.
- Having more faith in the Bible than in the Spirit of God or in Jesus.
- Pointing themselves and others toward anything but Jesus for salvation.
- Not talking about the power of the Spirit changing their lives.
- Not talking about how they have been led by the Spirit.

- Judging those outside Christ and talking about their failures.
- Justifying themselves by how much they do and get right.

Move Forward and Upward as a New Creation Through the Spirit

1. The Spirit of God, placed inside us, is a deposited miracle that acts upon our hearts and minds. He continues, just as He did in the early church, to give us signs and wonders pointing to Christ as He works to help us transform our lives. He still performs miracles in the world today.

2. The Spirit of God works in many ways and one of these is through our hearing and meditating upon Scripture. He reveals Christ and makes truth known to us.

3. The Spirit of God also works through others as He prompts their words of strength, encouragement and comfort that point us to God's power, peace and steadfast love for us. We also see Him revealed in nature and He may talk to us there or in our dreams or though signs just for us.

4. People are drawn toward God by the testimony of The Spirit upon their hearts and they are enabled by Him to hear the story of Jesus and the testimonies of changed lives. The Spirit may use any medium: facts, story, evidence from creation or the accounts of God's interaction in another person's life story—past or present. His methods of revelation are infinite in number.

5. Facts and testimonies about God and His Spirit working in the world today have a crucial place in discussions between brothers and sisters in Christ. A person's testimony through the Spirit has a profound effect on the people who hear them.

6. The Spirit of God will give us direction in our life if we look for it and as we remember to trust in the Lord with all our heart and to lean not on our own understanding as we acknowledge Him in all our ways and as He directs our paths.

7. The Spirit will convict, challenge and tell us if our feelings, behaviors or thoughts are wrong before and during the passing moments in life—if we stop and listen.

Don't Fall from Grace

It is for freedom that Christ has set us free. Stand firm, then, and do not let yourselves be burdened again by a yoke of slavery.

Mark my words! I, Paul, tell you that if you let yourselves be circumcised, Christ will be of no value to you at all. Again I declare to every man who lets himself be circumcised that he is obligated to obey the whole law. *You who are trying to be justified by law have been alienated from Christ; you have fallen away from grace.* But *by faith we eagerly await through the Spirit the righteousness for which we hope.* For in Christ Jesus neither circumcision nor uncircumcision has any value. *The only thing that counts is faith expressing itself through love.*

You were running a good race. Who cut in on you and kept you from obeying the truth? That kind of persuasion does not come from the one who calls you. "A little yeast works through the whole batch of dough." I am confident in the Lord that you will take no other view. The one who is throwing you into confusion will pay the penalty, whoever he may be. Brothers, if I am still preaching circumcision, why am I still being persecuted? In that case the offense of the cross has been abolished. As for those agitators, I wish they would go the whole way and emasculate themselves!

You, my brothers, were called to be free.

But do not use your freedom to indulge the sinful nature; rather, serve one another in love. The entire law is summed up in a single command: "Love your neighbor as yourself." If you keep on biting and devouring each other, watch out or you will be destroyed by each other.

So I say, live by the Spirit, and you will not gratify the desires of the sinful nature. For the sinful nature desires what is contrary to the Spirit, and the Spirit what is contrary to the sinful nature. They are in conflict with each other, so that you do not do what you want. But if you are led by the Spirit, you are not under law.

The acts of the sinful nature are obvious: sexual immorality, impurity and debauchery; idolatry and witchcraft; hatred, discord, jealousy, fits of rage, selfish ambition, dissensions, factions and envy; drunkenness, orgies, and the like. I warn you, as I did before, that those who live like this will not inherit the kingdom of God.

But the fruit of the Spirit is *love, joy, peace, patience, kindness, goodness, faithfulness, gentleness and self-control. Against such things there is no law.* Those who belong to Christ Jesus have crucified the sinful nature with its passions and desires. Since we live by the Spirit, let us keep in step with the Spirit. (Gal. 5:1–25)

Your faith saves you.
Rise up in His grace. Grow in grace. It is sufficient.
Express your faith through love.
Serve one another. Love your neighbor as yourself.
Live by the Spirit and you will gratify the Father's desires for you.
Pray unceasingly in all kinds of circumstances.
Keep in step with the Spirit.

This Week

- Please read Galatians again. As you do, please pray for the Spirit to reveal any code or law or principle you have followed, perhaps blindly, that has hindered the Spirit's work in you or in the churches you have attended. Write it down and pray for God to release you from this bondage.

- More importantly, please pray that God increases your faith and that He teaches you how to be led by His Spirit throughout each day. Ask Him to draw you close and teach you what is right or wrong in these lessons about the Spirit, and what He wants you to change about your beliefs, behaviors, faith or prayer life.

- Each day withdraw to a place of solitude and pray this: *Dear Lord, teach me to delight in you and then give me the desires of my heart.* ("Delight yourself in the LORD and he will give you the desires of your heart," Psa. 37:4) Interestingly, the desires He'll put within you will be good for you—always.

• • • •

May God bless you this week and may you be filled with His Spirit in all that you do. Peace be with you.

intimacy wanted in open fields of freedom . . .

A horse grazes in a field high up and in the mountains. The grandeur of God's beauty finds itself playing its spiritual music upon the streams cascading over rocks and the wind gently pushing the grasses and the horse's mane up and over his neck. He's free, but alone, and knows the saying "They Shoot Horses Don't They?" Often he glances about for predators and those that slide through the wheat and make themselves known only when upon his back. He stops. He looks. He lowers his head. He's alone whether with the others or by himself. He's alone. He longs to trust. He longs to spend some time with the one who cares about him—an owner maybe, who will watch over him yet lets him run free—but not too far and not in wrong places, but free to run and enjoy his life fully. Yet, now, he's always watchful. He doesn't know where He is or if He's real. But, he really wants Him.

People leave their homes looking for intimacy while living far apart even on the pews each Sunday—so near to others who also live remotely everywhere they go. How are they? "I'm fine," they say even occasionally with hugs. But are they? I know: I've sat on a pew and felt terrible and yet smiled anyway. Only one Maker can fill lives with joy and, for Christians, He lives inside, yet they look away, just like those before, to what destroys the life they want to live freely indeed (John 8:36).

> Like a horse in open country,
>> they did not stumble . . .
>> they were given rest by the
>>> Spirit of the Lord. (Is. 63:13–14)

5

WARNINGS AND GRIEVING THAT WILL STOP A MIRACLE 3

He walked for 8 hours up a mountain, from 800 feet to 3,400 feet above sea level, over 14 miles on a path through rocks and trees, and then he reached the summit. Looking down from the Mount of Olives, He saw the city. A cry, an uncontrollable wailing, rose from within him without warning as He approached the city of His Father's chosen people.

The centuries of travel and protection and compassionate concern flooded His mind and senses, and knowledge of the past, and the coming, destruction welled up from within Him, bursting from His heart. Memories of Abraham, Isaac, Jacob, Joseph, Moses, the Red Sea parting, manna in the desert, 40 years of wandering, and the promised land. Of battles and kings and judges and prophets. Of David and Solomon and the temple with the Holy of Holies along with continual rebellion and sin, pain and separation. And His own crucifixion and death and separation from the Father faced Him. Jesus wept over the city and said:

> If you, even you, had only known on this day what would bring you peace—but now it is hidden from your eyes. The days will come upon you when your enemies will build an embankment against you and encircle you and hem you in on every side. They will dash you to the ground, you and the children within your walls. They will not leave one stone on another, *because you did not recognize the time of God's coming to you.* (Luke 19:42–44)

After the death and resurrection of Jesus, Paul looked at those in the church of Galatia and called them bewitched and foolish. He condemned those leading them away from the Spirit of God and back to law and to a dependence on fleshly effort and to separation from God. He could see the walls crumbling, the enemy encircling and driving them to destruction and a fall from grace. Paul didn't cry. Instead, he was angry. That's why he wrote his letter to them using very harsh words.

Even in the olden days, the days of their rebellion, and the Father's acts of love and His many kindnesses, the Israelites rebelled and grieved His Holy Spirit. The apostle Paul knew the bad influence in Galatia was a sign of rebellion and separation from God. Having been educated at the school of Gamaliel with one of the most noted rabbis in history, He knew the Scriptures well. He had memorized the stories of the Old Testament and knew Isaiah's account of Israel's grieving of the Holy Spirit:

I will tell of the kindnesses of the LORD,
   the deeds for which he is to be praised,
   according to all the LORD has done for us—
yes, the many good things he has done
   for the house of Israel,
   according to his compassion and many kindnesses.
He said, "Surely they are my people,
   sons who will not be false to me";
   and so he became their Savior.
In all their distress he too was distressed,
   and the angel of his presence saved them.
In his love and mercy he redeemed them;
   he lifted them up and carried them
   all the days of old.
Yet they rebelled
   and grieved his Holy Spirit.
So he turned and became their enemy
   and he himself fought against them.

Then his people recalled the days of old,
   the days of Moses and his people—
where is he who brought them through the sea,
   with the shepherd of his flock?
Where is he who set
   his Holy Spirit among them,
who sent his glorious arm of power
   to be at Moses' right hand,
who divided the waters before them,
   to gain for himself everlasting renown,

who led them through the depths?
Like a horse in open country,
   they did not stumble;
like cattle that go down to the plain,
   they were given rest by the Spirit of the LORD.
(Is. 63:7–14)

Because they are preyed upon, horses don't easily trust and pursue intimate relationships with other animals or people. In the open country, they can see for miles. The light makes everything clear and danger, in its many forms, has difficulty approaching without making them aware.

It's not easy to get a horse to trust you. They can sense your emotions and intent, your anger, your fear or your uncertainty.

If we were horses in God's kingdom, He'd know if He'd gained our trust. That's because He would see us:

- Come to Him.
- Be at ease around Him.
- Follow His instructions.
- Respect Him.
- Allow Him to touch us.

And, then we would be like horses in open country running free, always rightly standing or moving, or at rest in the Spirit of the Lord (Is. 63:13–14).

At liberty, without a rope or halter, you know if a horse trusts you—if he loves you!

When he is free, will he look away in fear? Will he trust you fully? Will he follow you? Will he come to you and stay with you? Will he find joy in the freedom he has with you?

But, instead of freedom from fear, Jesus and Paul both discern the warnings of the impending destruction. They both witness these from different vantage points.

Jesus sees the money changers in the temple and the helpless people by the roadside begging for Him to touch them. He sees the religious people, the scripture Scripture bearers, who don't know God and will not come to Him. They disobey him. They disrespect Him. They will not allow Him to touch them. They lead others into a prison of condemnation.

Evil is growing in the land. Darkness lies over Jerusalem. Jesus' crucifixion is near. Satan wants His death. He'll soon separate Himself from God to take my sins, your sins—everybody's sins—upon Himself and die a terrible sacrificial death. Jesus looks out over the city and wails and moans over it.

When Paul sits down to write a letter to the Galatians, he's angry and tells them that he writes in LARGE LETTERS in his own hand.

> Grace and peace to you from God our Father and the Lord Jesus Christ, who gave himself for our sins to rescue us from the present evil age, according to the will of our God and Father, to whom be glory for ever and ever. Amen.
>
> I am astonished that you are so quickly deserting the one who called you by the grace of Christ and are turning to a different gospel— which is really no gospel at all. Evidently some people are throwing you into confusion and are trying to pervert the gospel of Christ. But even if we or an angel from heaven should preach a gospel other than the one we preached to you, *let him be eternally condemned!* . . .

> As we have already said, so now I say again: If any-
> body is preaching to you a gospel other than what you
> accepted, let him be *eternally condemned!* (Gal. 1:3–9)

Again, evil is present, seeking to pull the people away from Jesus and a trusting relationship with the Father. Evil wants to shroud His gift of becoming a new creation—each person transformed by the Spirit of God in them. This will grieve the Spirit and Paul knows it will make the church and its people impotent and helpless. Some of them may even fall from grace or not begin a transformed life in the Spirit. They will not experience the gift of Christ and the daily transforming power of the Holy Spirit. It will not matter how many scriptures they read or how much effort they apply. They will lose or never experience the fruit of the new covenant. They will wander lost—barely saved or not saved at all.

And so, Paul wishes that those bringing back law to them, bringing back a prison of legalism, should be emasculated and eternally condemned. Now, that's righteous anger!

As we journey through the Bible, Paul's letter of warning to the Galatians is followed by a letter to the saints in Ephesians. His first words explain to them his desires of grace and peace for them. He wants them to know they have been chosen to be holy and blameless in God's sight. He tells them they have been redeemed by the blood of Jesus, the forgiveness of their sins, and that a glorious grace has been given freely to them because of their faith. And that, with their belief, God marked them as in Christ. He marked them with the seal of the promised Holy Spirit. Now, the Spirit of God is their deposit guaranteeing their inheritance until the redemption of those who are God's possession—to the praise of His glory (Eph. 1:14).

Paul has been praying that God will give them the Spirit of *wisdom and revelation* (Eph. 1:17) so that they will know Jesus better. He also wants them *to know His great power* for those who believe—*a power that is like the working of His mighty strength* which He displayed in Christ's resurrection and ascension to His right hand in the heavenly realms (Eph. 1:19).

We were all dead in sin prior to our salvation in Christ Jesus. We lived to gratify our desires. We followed the ways of the world and the ruler of the kingdom of the air. He saved us by His grace, through our faith. Paul explains this occurred through faith—not from ourselves, it is the gift of God. Because of this we're eternally grateful and faithful to our new friend, Jesus, and can approach God with freedom and confidence.

We are a new creation, God's workmanship. We are created to do good works which have already been prepared for us to do. God has seated us with His Son in the heavenly realms and He is our peace. (Eph. 2:1-10)

Through Jesus we enjoy an intimate access to the Father by the Spirit. We are a dwelling in which God lives. We do not grieve the Holy Spirit of God, with whom we've been sealed. We follow and love Jesus.

This Week

- As you think about Paul's words to the Galatians, please continue to His next letter and read Ephesians. As you do, please pray that the Spirit provide you with wisdom and revelation about Himself and about the glorious gift of His Son. As you read, and the Spirit interacts with what you learn, *please write down what God and His Son have given you*.

- Also, *what is the Spirit teaching you through these lessons and why is this important at this time in your life*?

- More importantly, please pray that you know the wisdom and the revelation and the power of the Holy Spirit in your daily walk with the Father. Pray as you wake up and as you go to bed. Pray in the Spirit on all occasions with all kinds of prayers and requests. Pray unceasingly.

• • • •

May God bless you with truth, righteousness, readiness, good news, peace, faith, knowledge of your salvation, the word of God and the Spirit's revelation in your daily and prayer-filled walk with Him and His Son—Jesus.

nowhere else to go for help . . .

Several seasons ago there was a young man who went to one of the most prestigious baseball colleges in America. He was a pitcher and after years of Little League conferences and high school stardom he had made it. His time of hard work and playing in the dirt had earned him a place in one of the elite baseball programs in the country. But it ended there with his hopes and dreams.

He was now a salesman selling medical devices. His young son began to play baseball and he decided to coach. At each practice and after every game, he berated his child, pushed his child and criticized his child on the field and at home, alone and in front of others. His mom even went to the assistant coach, who was always encouraging the kids, and asked him to "Save my son!" But things didn't change and instead the coach got rid of his assistant. Criticisms of his son continued until the father was hit by a line drive in the head while throwing batting practice, which not only ended his coaching, but also his life as a salesman. He had to take disability and stay home. One day, when out eating, the previous assistant coach ran into him and, much to his surprise, was told, "You were right. I was wrong and out of line. Thank you."

There's a way that seems right to us today, but isn't. Some of us need to be hit hard to get our attention on Him. I pray that everyone who needs it, receives their Damascus experience either in a batting cage or at home or wherever, that they may be changed in an instant or in the years ahead.

6

HIS POWERFUL PURPOSE FOR THE BENEFIT OF PEOPLE

The Spirit of God wants to love you with the truth. He wants you to believe Him and, just like Abraham, He wants you to be a friend of God (Jas 2:23). He wants to walk with you and be your advocate—your helper. He wants to help shape your character and personality into the likeness of Christ Jesus.

He hovers over the darkness and the deep
over a world or a person in chaos—He weeps

The complaints rise up in the hardships of life
from a man or a woman or a husband or a wife

Is His arm too short or His words untrue
or is it bitterness and sin welling up in you

The Spirt of God comes upon whomever He may choose
and if we do not see or do not hear our lives we may lose

David's cry, his desire and his plea,
"Do not take your presence or your Holy Sprit from me!"

For when it comes time on that very important day
He'll give you knowledge of what you should say

He'll give you gifts and ability and skill
to make the world better in the way that He wills

He'll move you, fill you, come upon you and make you glad
with a word or a sign or some desire that He has

It's love and joy and patience and peace
or kindness and goodness at the very least

Faithfulness and gentleness and self-control
as He works and guides and powers us toward Jesus—His goal

So, as you believe in the one who is true
and give Him your heart—He lives in you

And He'll be with you to the very end of the age
as you witness to others no matter their age

Their lives forever saved in peace and in that hour
their resurrection insured by His great power

We now know why Paul is angry—why it matters to him that the people of Galatia are trying to attain their goal of righteousness by human effort—why it is crucial that they begin their transformation in the Spirit and not in their own effort. We can see it in Paul's past and in the story of his meeting with Jesus on the road to Damascus.

He is passionate about God's law—circumcised on the eighth day, of the people of Israel, of the tribe of Benjamin, a Hebrew of Hebrews; in regard to the law, a Pharisee; as for zeal, persecuting the church; as of legalistic righteousness, faultless. From a deep religious conviction of his own knowledge, of his own righteousness, of his own feelings, of his own power, Paul makes murderous criticisms and threats against the disciples of Christ. He writes letters to the high priest and asks for his permission to take Christian men and women to prison in Jerusalem.

Paul labors to destroy the church wherever he finds it. As an instrument of evil, he stands as a witness, giving his approval and watching stones thrown at Stephen, a man filled with the Spirit and God's grace and power. He watches until Stephen dies.

Then, without warning, on the road to Damascus, Jesus meets him and, with His words and the light of His holy presence, sweeps away all that Paul believes along with his former identity. Paul closes his eyes. He falls to the ground and hears this:

"Saul, Saul, why do you persecute me?"
"Who are you, Lord?" Saul asked.

> "I am Jesus, whom you are persecuting," He replied. "Now
> get up and go into the city, and you will be told what you
> must do." (Acts 9:4–6)

For three days, Paul is blind. He fasts. He does not eat or drink anything. In his encounter with the resurrected Christ, he sees the awful life he has led apart from God. In those first moments of understanding, repentance and belief in Jesus, and in the days and years afterward, Paul experiences mercy and grace. He receives an imperishable salvation by faith. He hears from Jesus, whom he's persecuted, and sees in Him the gift of His suffering, death and resurrection. Paul is a new creation in the Spirit, and has a new faith in God expressing itself in love and not in the letter of the law.

In the days ahead, Paul experiences freedom and compassion through the actions of Christ and the indwelling of the Spirit of God. Paul knows he is a child of God and a friend of Jesus.

That's why Paul writes with great force. He cries out to the Galatians as they allow others to convince them to separate themselves from the Spirit:

> I have been crucified with Christ and I no longer live, but
> Christ lives in me. The life I live in the body, I live by faith
> in the Son of God, who loved me and gave himself for me.
> I do not set aside the grace of God, for if righteousness
> could be gained through the law, Christ died for nothing!
> (Gal. 2:20–21)

Jesus saves Paul and puts him to work helping announce and advance the kingdom of God. With gladness, Paul gives up his former life—a strict and self-righteous life of ritualistic tradition and written law marked by:

Do this, do that, sacrifice lambs, spill blood over altars, feasts and fasting before God to wear this, stay away from that, do not touch, do not eat, work is this, work is that—escalated into no mercy man-made rules and treatments, stonings, murders, crucifixions, and a hypocritical life . . . pure, impure, arguments about the law, a new one here and there, a righteousness by steps and patterns and systems and words and miserable principles without fellowship for those who disagree—a reformation of behaviors, disciplines and salvation-earning practices splitting into fragments and sects of the only way . . . yet separated from God and without justice, mercy and faithfulness, and unable to recognize the good news of Jesus, the Messiah, a people unable to testify about Him and love Him and love the people around them.

Paul also surrenders his reputation and legalistic pride in exchange for the love of Jesus and a righteousness before God through faith—unearned, without an addendum or postscript; simply the good news, grace through faith. The notoriety of his former life, a zealous authority, a scholar and a warrior for the law and its rules and regulations, Paul now considers these to be worldly rubbish.

He sheds his old identity. He crucifies his past. The old Paul no longer lives. Instead he gains Christ, Christ living in him. He gains freedom from condemnation. He gains life to the full—with the Spirit of God living in him.

Jesus, with nails in His hands and feet, hangs from a cross and dies for all of Paul's sins—sacrificing Himself to bring him eternal life. Paul believes in this act of Christ, in his own salvation by faith.

Jesus gives Paul the Spirit for his work and to give life to his mortal body, to lead him and to help him put to death the misdeeds of the body, to help in his weakness, to testify with the Spirit that he's God's child. And, Paul cries, just as we cry, "Abba, Father!" Amazing grace.

When Paul sees the new children of Christ in Galatia being taken from their Father, from Christ and the Spirit, he erupts in protective anger at their teachers. He wants these "perverters" removed, emasculated and eternally condemned. His anger is similar to that of how Jesus reacted to the Pharisees before His death.

Jesus, as He weeps over Jerusalem, and Paul as he vents his anger, both experience the same concern—a separating of a person, or people, from the Father, causing the loss of their first love.

As we read in the Galatian story, Paul saw people he loved being pulled away from God. He saw them listening to a bewitching influence, their hearts being carried into a foolish separation from their heavenly Father and toward a fall from grace.

They were depending upon themselves to earn salvation and not upon Christ's work and the Spirit's daily presence.

They were abandoning the cross and the Savior's suffering, death and resurrection for them and instead were beginning to rely on themselves.

Paul knew the love of Jesus because of his own merciful experience on the road to Damascus. Jesus died for him. He freed him, the worst of all, from a fleshly, effort-filled life of bondage and from a spiritual deadness. Jesus gave him life everlasting, and the daily transformational filling of the Holy Spirit. Understanding and experiencing this remarkable gift from the Father made Paul angry toward those leading the Galatians back into bondage. He realized they were being steered away from a salvation by faith and away from the mercy and grace of the Messiah and the precious advocacy of the Holy Spirit.

The Spirit Loves Us with Truth

Into your hands I commit my spirit;
   redeem me, O LORD, the God of truth.
   (Psa. 31:5)

Surely you desire truth in the inner parts;
   you teach me wisdom in the inmost place.
   (Psa. 51:6)

But when he, the Spirit of truth, comes, he will guide you into all truth. He will not speak on his own; he will speak only what he hears, and he will tell you what is yet to come. (John 16:13)

Jesus answered, "I am the way and the truth and the life. No one comes to the Father except through me." (John 14:6)

We need Jesus. We need His love and truth to guide us each day. We need the Spirit to reveal Him and His direction for our lives. We need this for ourselves and our children. We need this when we wake up and when we go to bed. We need the Spirit of God to direct our path as people, as a family, and as a fellowship and church. We cannot live without the Spirit. We live, really live, only with Him.

This Week

- Please read John 14 and through the prayer of Jesus to the end of chapter 17. Before you do this, please ask God by His Spirit to reveal what He wants you to hear and then write these things down. You may want to read this passage of Scripture at least three times in the next week and to pray each time asking Him to speak to you through His words.

- At this point in your life, describe your relationship with the Spirit of God. As you write, think about what Jesus says of Him in His prayer (John 14).

- What are ways you could be grieving or quenching the Spirit's work and influence upon your life? Do you need to be filled with the Spirit? Do you need Him to remove what keeps you from being filled?

  Ananias was sent to Paul so that he could see again and be filled with the Holy Spirit. Later, Paul prays as I pray for all of us, "May the God of hope fill you with all joy and peace as you trust in him, so that you may overflow with hope by the power of the Holy Spirit" (Rom. 15:13).

· · · ·

Part II

TRANSFORMATION
IN THE SPIRIT

streams of new beginnings . . .

In the beginning God created, He laid the foundations of the earth. In the beginning was the word and the word was with God and the word was God. The Spirit of God hovered over the waters.

In the beginning, a man started a garden in the direction of the early morning sun. But, having never been taught what was right, he grew his plants without water and continued to do this over and over and over again as each one he cared for withered and died—until he began to lose confidence in how he had started. His days were painful toil with dying parts of himself lying around on the ground. Some of the broken pieces he carried with him were those of shame, self-loathing, anxiety, and depression, and he carried them beside his failures in a wheelbarrow of dead branches.

As he reached the end of his abilities, he closed his eyes and died and was born again into a new creation. Every day was a fresh new beginning, and his new family gave him streams of living water that ran through his heart growing lots of vibrant tomatoes and apples and fresh figs.

In the morning, O LORD, you hear my voice in the morning I lay my requests before you and wait in expectation. (Psa. 5:3)

Every morning is a new beginning in the Spirit of God.

7

BEGINNING A NEW LIFE
IN THE SPIRIT

Isaiah, hundreds of years before Christ, told us that God would pour out His Spirit and His blessing. Ezekiel prophesied that God would give us an undivided heart and put a new spirit in us; and He'd remove from us our hearts of stone and give us a heart of flesh by *putting His Spirit in us to move us to follow* His decrees and to be careful to keep His laws (Ezek. 36:26–27).

Joel also tells us:
And afterward, I will pour out my Spirit on all people.

Your sons and daughters will prophesy,
your old men will dream dreams,
your young men will see visions.

Even on my servants, both men and women, I will pour out my Spirit in those days (Joel 2:28–29).

And, best of all, Jeremiah's words,

"The time is coming," declares the LORD,
    "when I will make a new covenant
with the house of Israel
    and with the house of Judah.
It will not be like the covenant
    I made with their forefathers
when I took them by the hand
    to lead them out of Egypt,
because they broke my covenant,
    though I was a husband to them,"
declares the LORD.
"This is the covenant I will make with the house of Israel
    after that time," declares the Lord.
"I *will put my law in their minds*
    and write it on their hearts.
I will be their God,
    and they will be my people.
No longer will a man teach his neighbor,
    or a man his brother, saying, 'Know the LORD,'
because they will all know me,
    from the least of them to the greatest,"
declares the LORD.
"For I will forgive their wickedness
    and will remember their sins no more."
(Jer. 31:31–35)

Amazing grace, sins forgiven and not remembered, and the Spirit poured out on us with prophecies, dreams and visions; the Spirit moving us, leading us, reminding us and teaching us about Jesus.

An inspired life!

We know that the Spirit of God moves upon the darkness and He brings peace to the disorder He finds there. He does this with a truth-revealing light and by revealing Jesus and He does this in the world by moving within those who love His Son.

The Father fills believers with His Spirit, and with skills, ability and knowledge, and all kinds of gifts in music, lyrics, singing, dancing, carpentry, cooking, leading, serving and teaching.

For we are all God's workmanship created in Christ Jesus to do good works which God prepared for us to do (Eph. 2:10) for the benefit of those He brings to us and for His glory.

The Lord put His Spirit upon Moses (Num. 11:17) and rested on others as they prophesied (Num. 11:25). He came upon Gideon (Judg. 6:34) and David (1 Sam. 16:13) and Samson (Judg. 15:14) in power, and battles were won and lions torn apart. He made those who were weak or weakened in the eyes of the world bold and ambitious for righteousness (Matt. 5:3–10).

The Spirit came upon Saul (1 Sam. 11:6), and then after a time of rebellion and sin, He left him (1 Sam. 16:14) and remained with a man after God's own heart, David (1 Sam. 16:13).

Isaiah prophesied that the Spirit of God would rest on Jesus:

> the Spirit of wisdom and of understanding
> the Spirit of counsel and of power
> the Spirit of knowledge and of the fear of the LORD.
> (Is. 11:2)

> For to us a child is born, to us a son is given; and the government will be upon His shoulders, and He will be called Wonderful Counselor, Mighty God, Everlasting Father, Prince of Peace. (Is. 9:6)

Jesus.

The Prince of Peace Leaves Us a Miraculous Gift

When Jesus, a man, who is one with God and is God, nears His death and return to heaven, His last words are measured with the understanding that His followers will be left alone and looking for guidance and direction. Here are a few things He tells them:

- Their faith will cause them to do even greater things than He has done (John 14:12).
- What they ask for He'll do (Mark 11:24).
- The Spirit of truth, the Counselor, will be with them and in them forever (John 15:26; 16:13).
- He's in the Father and they'll be in Him and He in them (John 17:21).

- The Spirit will teach them all things and remind them of His teachings (John 14:26).
- Apart from Him, they can do nothing (John 15:5).
- To remain in Him and love each other as He has loved them (John 15:6).
- This is His command: Love each other (John 15:12).
- The Spirit will testify about Him and they must also testify (John 15:26–27).

The Spirit will convict the world in regard to sin and righteousness and judgment (John 16:8).
The Spirit will guide them into all truth (John 16:13).
The Spirit will bring glory to Jesus (John 16:14).
The Spirit will take what is from Jesus and make it known to them (John 16:14).

Jesus prays for them and for those who will believe in Him through their message, that they will be one because of the glory He gives them and that God gave Him. He prays that they will be brought into complete unity. And He finally finishes His heartfelt and earnest pleading before God with these words:

Father, I want those you have given me to be with me where I am, and to see my glory, the glory you have given me because you loved me before the creation of the world.

Righteous Father, though the world does not know you, I know you, and they know that you have sent me.

I have made you known to them, and will continue to make you known in order that the love you have for me may be in them and that I myself may be in them. (John 17:24–26)

How Did You Begin Your Life with Jesus?

Please look back into the story of your salvation—the one you would testify about. Were you saved by the grace of God through faith in Jesus?

Did you begin by believing in Jesus as your Lord and as the Son of God? Did you believe in the good news—His death for your sins to make you righteous before God? Did you accept His grace and receive His salvation?

Did you begin your reborn life in the Spirit? Or did you do any of these?

- Live with the Spirit quenched and grieved within you as you tried to change yourself by your own effort?
- Begin in faith but without a knowledge of the Spirit within you?
- Bounce back and forth between trusting God, especially during difficult times, and relying on yourself during better times?
- Do what was expected at church, attendance, and so on, and then continue a flesh-aided and unsaved life without belief and without much testimony of a change in your character and personality and without evidence of being reborn—remaining pretty much the same over the years?

- Continue in an unsaved state and in willful disobedience and sin?

Can you tell those around you about how the Spirit has reshaped you into the likeness of Jesus Christ? Can you describe your battles with the flesh, and your prayerful resistance and the victories empowered and won by the Spirit of God within you? In other words, that your former self no longer lives? That you're a better person and more in love with Jesus?

Do people see more of these within you than they did in your past life: love, joy, peace, patience, kindness, goodness, faithfulness, gentleness and self-control?

Today, are you filled with the Spirit of God or do you need Him to flame a fire within you? Do you marvel at His presence in your life and what He does for you and how He strengthens, encourages and comforts you? Do you find yourself praying during all kinds of occasions? Do you thank Him and praise Him in good times and in bad?

Are you a saint? Are you God's child—a prince or princess of the King? Are you a friend of Jesus?

Do not put out the Spirit's fire . . .

May God himself, the God of peace, sanctify you through and through. May your whole spirit, soul and body be kept blameless at the coming of our Lord Jesus Christ. (1 Th. 5:19, 23)

This Week

- Please test everything you read and hear in this study with prayer and a careful study of the words of God within the Bible. Ask the Father for the Spirit to lead you to what you need to know and to guard your mind from the leading of any other spirit.

- No matter where you are with Jesus, whatever the sin, He'll meet you there without condemnation. Offer Him your heart in prayer this week and ask Him to fill you with His Spirit and continue His work within you.

- Please remember, "You however, are controlled not by the sinful nature but by the Spirit, if the Spirit of God lives in you. And if anyone does not have the Spirit of Christ, he does not belong to Christ" (Rom. 8:9).

If you didn't accept Jesus into your life by faith, and you believe in Him now, and you want His salvation now, then, in prayer, give your life to Him. If you wish, I would be glad to be your witness and take you through this moment in prayer. If not me, please find someone who will hear your testimony.

• • • •

childlike trust and wonder . . .

A man was walking down his long driveway in the country with his dog behind him when he saw a young lamb standing there. It must have wandered from a neighboring farm. He rushed to pick it up because he was afraid of what his farm dog might do to it.

That's when it happened, when the lamb was in his arms, an unforeseen moment of awe, for he had never held an animal so innocent and beautiful, so guiltless, so blameless, so pure. A lamb. As pure and blameless as a newborn baby needing security, needing refuge, needing safekeeping, needing love.

Our childhoods, our innocence, are gone. In our genes, we bear the sins of our fathers to the third and fourth generation. The lamb of God wants us to put away childish things and take on our brokenness with repentance and submission. And He wants us to do this with childlike faith and wonderment, so that the Father will see us as beautiful, guiltless, blameless and pure. He will then take us up in the Spirit and into His arms. He will protect us from the powers and principalities. He will love us, once again, as His perfect children.

Let the little children come to me,
and do not hinder them, for the
kingdom of heaven belongs to
such as these. (Matt. 19-14)

8

DON'T GRIEVE THE SPIRIT WITHIN YOU

The Jewish people had been waiting hundreds of years for the appearance of the Messiah and His new kingdom. They believed He'd save them from their present circumstances under the Romans just as they had been freed from a life of slavery under the Egyptians. The anointed one would come in power. He'd establish a kingdom for their redemption and safety, and they would be brought back into their former glory.

He came in a manger.

When it was His time to establish His kingdom, He chose young prostitutes, tax collectors and fishermen with whom to build His army—His band of followers. As He neared the cross, many of them denied and abandoned Him.

Where did He form His kingdom? What were its boundaries? What were the requirements for entrance? Where was its glory?

Once, having been asked by the Pharisees when the kingdom of God would come, Jesus replied, "The kingdom of God does not come with your careful observation, nor will people say, 'Here it is,' or 'There it is,' *because the kingdom of God is within you."* (Luke 17:20–21)

When Jesus saw this, he was indignant. He said to them, "Let the little children come to me, and do not hinder them, for the kingdom of God belongs to such as these. I tell you the truth, *anyone who will not receive the kingdom of God like a little child will never enter it."* (Mark 10:14–15)

Faith and Belief in Jesus and the Father and the Spirit

Children enter this world with little fear toward anything. I remember standing my son Ryan up on my shoulders when he was about 3 years old. As I held on to his ankles, he'd dive out into the room trusting that I would keep him safe. He first flew out and then in an arc toward the ground and then swung between my legs, and with the momentum swung back and forth—laughing as he moved through the air. Jesus tells us that anyone who receives the kingdom of God like a little child will enter it; and, that when they do, they will find the kingdom is within them. I've seen many men and women over the years smile when they receive and find God and His Spirit within them.

The kingdom of God is within you—by your belief in Jesus. Previously, the ruler of the kingdom of the air was at work in you and in your disobedience. Now, God and Jesus live in you through the Holy Spirit. When the kingdom of God entered you, you were born again—first from the waters of your mother's womb, and the second time in the Spirit. What a miracle!

The New International Version of the Bible uses the word "faith" 246 times, with 231 of these references being in the New Testament. The word "believe" is used 150 times and 130 of these are in the New Testament. In these last days, the words of God and His testimonies and prophecies focus on our faith in Jesus. The new covenant and the good news declare that we'll be saved by our belief in Jesus as our Lord and Savior. Here are some verses to help us reflect on the importance of a person's faith:

- "[Y]our faith has healed you" (Matt. 9:22, Mark 5:34, 52; Luke 8:48).
- "According to your faith will it be done to you" (Matt. 9:29).
- "Woman, you have great faith! Your request is granted" (Matt. 15:28).
- "Your faith has saved you; go in peace" (Luke 7:50).
- "Increase our faith!" (Luke 17:5).
- "Rise and go; your faith has made you well" (Luke 17:19).
- "He was a good man, *full of the Holy Spirit and faith,* and a great number of people were brought to the Lord" (Acts 11:24).
- "He listened to Paul as he was speaking. Paul looked directly at him, *saw that he had faith to be healed,* and called out, 'Stand on your feet!' . . . the man jumped up and began to walk" (Acts 14:9–10).

- "And *without faith it is impossible to please God*, because anyone who comes to him must believe that he exists and that he rewards those who earnestly seek him" (Heb. 11:6).
- "And *he did not do many miracles there because of their lack of faith*" (Matt. 13:58).

And, one about unbelief . . .

- "'It has often thrown him into fire or water to kill him. But if you can do anything, take pity on us and help us.' "'If you can'?' said Jesus. 'Everything is possible for him who believes.' "Immediately the boy's father exclaimed, *'I do believe; help me overcome my unbelief!'*" (Mark 9:24).

When we depend upon anything but God, upon our image, intellect, power or relationships with others, we set up idols in our hearts and stumbling blocks in our lives. When the prophet Ezekiel addressed this, he spoke of a question God would ask, "Should I let them inquire of me at all?" (Ezek. 14:3). His answer, "I the Lord will answer them myself in keeping with their great idolatry. I will do this to recapture the hearts of the people . . . who have deserted me for their idols" (Ezek. 14:4–5). We also read that Jonah believed, "Those who cling to worthless idols forfeit the grace that could be theirs" (Jon. 2:8).

Just as it is "easier for a camel to go through the eye of a needle than for a rich man to enter the kingdom of God" (Matt. 19:24), this also applies if the riches are pride, power, control or our own understanding. We need to be the children of God that we are and trust our Father with everything, because just as Paul, we no longer live but Christ lives in us (Gal. 2:20). And the life we live in the body we live by faith in the Son of God, who loved us and gave himself for us.

So, do not set aside the grace of God. Gain your righteousness by faith and live each day in the Spirit and by your belief in Him, and the presence of Jesus and the Father within you. Depend on their strength, their encouragement, their comfort and their presence. Trust in the Spirit's leading with all your heart. Do not lean on your own understanding. Acknowledge God in all you do and He will direct your paths and they will be the best ones to take (Prov. 3:5–6). Live by faith.

Years ago, Robert Frost wrote my favorite poem, "The Road Not Taken." In it he tells of the choices of life that we all face, and that as we look back we see the impact of the decisions we make. "Two roads diverged in a yellow wood, and sorry I could not travel both and be one traveler." As the traveler thinks of his life, he ends his poem by telling us, "Two roads diverged in a wood, and I— I took the one less traveled by, and that has made all the difference."

When we're led by the ruler of the air, or by our own desires and our own understanding, and not by the Spirit of God, we grieve Him. Our absence and behaviors distress Him with sorrow and pain. When we do this, He lets us go off on our own and life without Him disciplines us. He then waits for our return.

In a deeper way, we grieve Him with our unloving behaviors toward our brothers and sisters: bitterness, rage, anger, slander and all forms of malice. There must not even be a hint of sexual immorality or any kind of impurity, or of greed—no obscenity, foolish talk or coarse joking, but rather thanksgiving. Paul tells us not to get drunk on wine, which leads to debauchery. Instead, he tells us to be filled with the Spirit and to "Speak to one another with psalms, hymns and spiritual songs. Sing and make music in your heart to the Lord, always giving thanks to God the Father for everything, in the name of our Lord Jesus Christ" (Eph. 4:31; 5:3–4, 18–20).

Filled with the Spirit of God

Each day has its challenges and decisions, mundane or significant moments and our response to them. These can be as simple as a discussion with a son, a daughter or a friend. We can start and end the day in prayer or with coffee and television. We can watch or say this or that. We can acknowledge God in some of these, none of these or all of these, or in some level in between. The Spirit is always with us. He may be quenched and grieved, but He's with us, yet we limit our access to Him.

Throughout the Bible, we read about the children of God being filled with the Holy Spirit:

"All of them were filled with the Holy Spirit" (Acts 2:4).

"Then Peter, filled with the Holy Spirit" (Acts 4:8).

"After they prayed, the place where they were meeting was shaken. And they were all filled with the Holy Spirit and spoke the word of God boldly" (Acts 4:31).

"They chose Stephen, a man full of faith and of the Holy Spirit" (Acts 6:5).

"Then Ananias went to the house and entered it. Placing his hands on Saul, he said, 'Brother Saul, the Lord—Jesus, who appeared to you on the road as you were coming here—has sent me so that you may see again and be filled with the Holy Spirit'" (Acts 9:17).

"He was a good man, full of the Holy Spirit and faith, and a great number of people were brought to the Lord" (Acts 11:24).

"[T]he disciples were filled with joy and with the Holy Spirit" (Acts 13:52).

"May the God of hope fill you with all joy and peace as you trust in him, so that you may overflow with hope by the power of the Holy Spirit" (Romans 15:13).

"[B]e filled with the Spirit" (Eph. 5:18).

We know how to live life during the week without any acknowledgment of the Spirit of God or without prayer to our Father. We get caught up in our own spirit and in the system of the world orchestrated by our fleshly desires and those of the ruler of the kingdom of the air. When this occurs, we're in need of revival—revival of our love for God and for Jesus and the Spirit's work in us.

We need to be renewed and restored in our passions for the King of kings. We need to be filled with joy and with the Spirit of God so that we trust in Him, find our peace in Him and overflow with hope. We need to have ourselves shaken from the forces against us and we need to speak boldly and testify of our love for Jesus and we need to do this filled with kindness and gentleness.

We don't need to behave with criticism, anger, timidity or pride. We need to repent and to have our lives changed from those things over which we cannot control ourselves. We need to be sanctified by the Holy Spirit and we need to be filled with His power within us for our own benefit, the benefit of others and the glory of God. We need to be filled with His Spirit and the love of Jesus.

This Week

- Find a quiet place and release to God any unsurrendered parts of your life. Ask Him to make you aware of your need for Him. Please ask the Father for your restoration. Ask Him to fill you with His Spirit and a renewed love for Jesus. Ask Him to fill you with hope and peace.

- If you need help with any of the above, please ask someone to pray for and with you.

- Are you filled with the Spirit and His hope and peace within you or have you lived without Him in your life. Your body is His temple and He wants to fill you with the truth about Jesus. You are a child of God and it doesn't matter how you feel about this at the present; it only matters what He says about His thoughts of you. He loves you. If this is hard for you to believe, ask Him to overcome your unbelief. "And *so we know and rely on the love God has for us. God is love.* Whoever lives in love lives in God, and God in him" (1 John 4:16).

Again, please remember Paul's prayer "May the God of hope fill you with all joy and peace *as you trust in him*, so that you may overflow with hope *by the power of the Holy Spirit*" (Rom. 15:13).

• • • •

passions placed well in Him . . .

We see them on Saturdays with painted faces eating and drinking outside their coliseums before the time of battle. For weeks, the drama of "if only thoughts" and agony and defeat and victories fill the airwaves. They worry and read about their favorites in the social media haunts they frequent. Their passions spill out into the seats during and after "the games," as they scream and drink their way into the night and the early morning. Each week they read and devour the words they find around the gladiators they love, knowing their choice of weapons, their possible strategies for victory, and what they may do to avoid embarrassment or death by defeat. Then Sunday comes and their passion leaves them. Some even stay at home because of late nights and depressive hangovers. The others sit in the pews dutifully singing and waiting through their spiritual obligations until the appointed time has ended and lunch begins.

Yet . . . Jesus, the author and perfecter of our faith, for the joy set before Him endured the cross, scorning its shame and sat down at the right hand of the throne of God. That's why each day and on Sunday the remnant fix their eyes on Him. With shouts and the sound of trumpets, they dance and leap before the Lord, singing psalms, hymns and spiritual songs with gratitude in their hearts to God. Others go to Him in silent prayer and praise. All of them seek Him eagerly and He is found by them. He is in them. He is their passion. He is their hope. He is their Lord.

> I have been crucified with Christ and
> I no longer live, but Christ lives in me.
> The life I live in the body, I live by faith
> in the Son of God, who loved me and
> gave himself for me. (Gal. 2:20)

9

BE VIGILANT TO PROTECT THE LIFE WITHIN YOU

A 6-year-old boy, just a young child, gets in the car with his mother on the way to their first day of school. He's dressed—his lunchbox with him.

As they approach the school, they get into a line of cars moving toward the school entrance at a cautious speed. When they reach the front door, the mom glances over at the seat beside her as her son gets out. She wants to hug him, but declines. She wants to cry with pride and joy, but controls her tears.

He gets out and, without looking back, walks into the school.

The tears and the emotions and the questions cascade down her cheeks and across her mind. He's gone! What will he learn on his first day? Will he make friends? How will his teacher treat him? What will he learn? Will he be harmed? Will he be OK when he returns home? Have I prepared him well for this day?

As shepherds and children of God with gifted ministries, please keep careful watch for possible dangers or difficulties in your daily walk with the Spirit. Begin with yourselves as Paul explained to the elders of the church at Ephesus: "Keep watch over yourselves and all the flock of which the Holy Spirit has made you overseers" (Acts 20:28.)

All of us should remember the warning to the Ephesian Christians, whom the Spirit described as having these strengths: deeds, hard work, perseverance, testing false teachers, enduring hardships for the name of Jesus, and having not grown weary. Yet, this was held against them:

> You have forsaken your first love. Remember the height from which you have fallen! Repent and do the things you did at first. If you do not repent, I will come to you and remove your lampstand from its place. (Rev. 2:4–5)

As the chapters in this study unfold, search the days behind you, your present and your thoughts for the future. Release these into the Spirit's care. Trust in the Lord with all your heart and all you do and think.

Turn away from doing things in your own effort and practice listening to the Spirit both within you and when He speaks through a brother or sister in Christ. Be filled with the Spirit and He'll fill you with your first love—Jesus.

If you need to, rekindle your love with an understanding of His love for you (Phil. 4:6). Walk in the freedom of His grace and love. "Love the Lord your God with all your heart and with all your soul and with all your strength and with all your mind" (Luke 10:27). In His presence, you will find no condemnation.

Then, shepherd and teach and serve everyone—especially those just beginning a new life with Jesus. Make sure, by your words and example, that you teach them how to live and walk with the Spirit of God. Talk about His goodness and mercy and grace and movement in your life and the life of the church. Do this at any time the Spirit prompts you to declare the glory of God.

Protect the life within you and within others. Don't allow zeal for ritualistic and legal righteousness or for the world's idolatry into your home, your workplace or the church . . . "Be careful," Jesus warns. "Watch out for the yeast of the Pharisees and that of Herod" (Mark 8:15). This means that we teach with kindness and clarity what the Bible says and do this in the Spirit and with real and personal examples—the bad and the good. We talk about how He's led us and our failures in walking without Him and our victories through Him.

To keep from disqualifying ourselves from this important work, especially remember to live out and teach these three spiritual concerns:

- *Identity*: Our New Names and Life of Freedom from Condemnation
- *Submission*: Living in the Spirit and Not in Rebellion Apart from God
- *Zeal*: The Protection of Our Homes, Families and Body Consumes Us

Identity: Our New Names and a Life Free from Condemnation

When the Spirit of God comes to live in us, He speaks to us about Jesus and tells us about our adoption into God's family (Rom. 8:15–16). By Him we cry, "Abba, Father." Daddy! Did you know that you're now this close to God—something unheard of in the Jewish nation? It's true!

We're His beloved children regardless of our past. We're sons and daughters of God and now live without fear. As we allow the Spirit to control our lives, we are at peace and streams of living water flow through us. This is the gift of God to those who believe. It is an amazing gift of grace. We are the children of *Yahweh*—a name rabbinical Judaism teaches as forbidden to say except by the High Priest in the Holy of Holies of the temple in Jerusalem!

The curtain has been torn in two by Jesus and we have been swept into the presence of the Lord. His temple and His Spirt are within us. We are dearly loved.

For some people, this is hard to accept. They hear or read that God loves them, but feel unforgiven and unloved. This occurs because of their past sins or how others have labeled them.

At times, even their parents or spouses or friends or classmates have treated them with contempt and have said "You'll never amount to much," or "You're ugly" or "You're stupid." Over time, these while not true, have become true in their minds. The Spirit of God can heal these wounds.

Men hurt women and women hurt men. We live in a defiant world of broken people hurting one another, labeling one another and living apart from God. In this environment, we receive the scars of the self-protective pride and rebellion we've lived with in the past. We then measure ourselves by many types of worthless weights and calculators—money, reputation, power, sexual conquest, titles, knowledge. With these, we place value stickers on our hearts and clothing which drive us to accumulate them more and more—always fearful, always vain, always uncertain, always unfulfilled, always comparing and never satisfied.

If you have done this, as I have, repent and allow yourself to trust Jesus. Remember, "the only thing that counts is faith expressing itself through love—a new creation" (Gal. 5:6; 6:15). Especially, know this—Jesus died on an ugly and demeaning cross to show you how much the Father loves you and, when you believe in Him, you become a dearly loved, bled for, child of God—a son or daughter of the KING.

In 2018, Lauren Daigle, with Jason Ingram and Paul Mabury, wrote the song "You Say," It broke all records for a Billboard #1 listing—over 100 weeks. Here is what she says about the song:

> "I knew this would be a song of my identity," she says. "'You say I am loved.' That's the truth." As for the album, Daigle says, "I want this to be such a record of joy, such a record of hope, that people experience a childlikeness again. In the time of making this record, I had to remember who I was as a child. I want people to reflect on, 'The innocence of my childhood . . . how do I see myself through those eyes again? How do I love myself like that again? Where's that joy? Where's that hope?'" ("Lauren Daigle on New

Album 'Look Up Child' & Single 'You Say': 'I Want This to
Be a Record of Joy & Hope'".*Billboard*.)

Why, in today's times, has this song been played billions
of times for those who believe in Jesus and for those who
don't? It's because many people in the world want to know
why they matter. They are confused and don't know, really
know, that God loves them especially when they hurt, or when
they feel weak or when they fall short of perfection. With their
song, Daigle, Ingram and Mabury help us see that people fight
voices that tell them they are not enough, that they will never
measure up. The person in the song wants God to remind
them of their identity.

If we just look around us, we see anxiety, suicide increases,
bullying and an amazing and powerful desire for being seen
and cared about. People are struggling to belong, to have
worth. Instagram, Facebook and TikTok apps feed this and
earn billions from these desires. In the song "You Say," people
hear the truth—that the only one thing that matters, when life
hurts and we feel worthless, is to know that in every situation
we face, and at every moment, God thinks of you and me as
His beloved children.

Yahweh loves you—you! Through His Spirit you know this
is true. Close your eyes and see Jesus dying for you. Believe
in your new identity: a child of God (John 1:12), a saint, a
holy one set apart for a divine purpose (Eph 1:1), Christ's
friend (John 15:5). And don't grieve the Spirit with any of
the previous labels of your old life! Accept the truth and live
as if you're loved and Jesus is the first love of your new life!

You are a Prince or Princess of the KING—the son or the daughter of God!

Submission: Living in the Spirit and Not Apart from God in Rebellion

What if you knew your child was walking into school, leaving the safety of your protection, and facing harm on the inside. That despite your love for him and your instruction, he'd no longer choose home or choose you? What would you do? Would you let him out of the car? Would you let him go?

When we stepped into the world, God let us go.

In the beginning, God created us and Eden to enjoy life together there. He made us a little lower than the angels and gave us dominion over the earth and the freedom to explore and live with Him in His newly created world. His only instructions were to produce, provide and take care of it and to stay away from one tree.

That tree—He knew we would choose it and He knew we would die. He knew we would rebel and He knew some in His heavenly court would as well. He knew the fallen heavenly beings would hurt us, draw us away from Him and teach us to hurt each other. He knew this, but let us go anyway.

His heart was filled with pain as He watched us choose idols and fallen gods over Him, as He witnessed our contempt for the created order and for Him, as He saw how great human wickedness on the earth had become, and that every inclination of the thoughts of human hearts was only evil all the time. He was filled with emotional pain in His heart—grieved that He had made humankind (Gen. 6:6).

The flood stopped this rebellion for only a few years. Then, He chose Israel to begin to reestablish His kingdom on earth—to guide a chosen nation, to protect, teach and make them ready for the coming of His Son.

Soon they grieved Him and His Holy Spirit as well—choosing idols over His deliverance from slavery in Egypt. They grumbled and rebelled after they escaped and while they journeyed through the desert to the promised land of Canaan.

In Jerusalem, time and again, they didn't trust Him. They went off on their own and into harm and back to enslavement and a miserable existence. Yet, after years of anguish, they would cry out to Him from the depths of their depravity and imprisonment by the nations and He'd save them and bring them home.

Finally, Jesus left heaven and lived as one of them. He lived a sinless life and became the final sacrifice. He died on a cross. He died for them and sent His Spirit to set up the kingdom of God, the rule of God and the love of God within every man or woman who believes.

Today, we rejoice and with joy live in the Spirit. We can smell home and feel the freedom of the living waters within us. We see the beauty of the created order, the love of the Father. It's near—very near. We'll soon be there, yet for a while we're still here within the broken world in service to the King of kings—our friend and our brother, our Savior and our Lord, Jesus.

By His power, we will not walk away. We will not rebel. He chose us to save us, and we will remember His sacrifice and His temple within us. We will gladly make ourselves a spectacle for His Glory and put away the things that harm us as we serve Him and those He brings into our presence.

We will bring others to Him and into His kingdom and His peace. He lives in us and we in Him for the purpose of redeeming the world. Our old nature no longer rules in this endeavor as we submit ourselves in faith to the Messiah.

We strive not to grieve the Holy Spirit of God with whom we've been sealed for the day of redemption. We do our best not to fill Him with pain. We do not separate ourselves from the love of Christ and the Father and the Spirit within us for we are . . .

> convinced that neither death nor life, neither angels nor demons, neither the present nor the future, nor any powers, neither height nor depth, nor anything else in all creation, will be able to separate us from the love of God that is in Christ Jesus our Lord. (Rom. 8:38–39)

Some in the church have lived defeated and prideful lives separated from others who love Jesus as Lord but who live in other houses of worship with different names. They have shut themselves off from the world and have become judgmental, focused on orthodoxy and systems instead of their first love—Jesus.

If you have done this in the past, as I have done, repent and continue to remember what Paul said "The only thing that counts is faith [in Jesus] expressing itself through love." (Gal. 5:6).

Especially, know this—Jesus died to show us how much the Father loves us and, when we believe in Him, we become a dearly loved, bled for, child of God—a son or daughter of the KING. Therefore, we will unify as one body, in the Spirit and in deed, with all our brothers and sisters across the world, to save the world! As much as it depends on us, we will not separate from others within God's family and grieve the Holy Spirit.

Zeal: The Protection of Our Homes, Families and Body Consumes Us

Never be lacking in zeal, but keep your spiritual fervor, serving the Lord. (Rom. 12:11) (Note: Zeal (zeō) means to "seethe," "boil," "be fervent in spirit.")

Jesus visits the temple courts in Jerusalem and finds men selling cattle, sheep and doves, and others sitting at tables exchanging money. Off by Himself, He twists cords and with wood-working skill makes a whip. He goes back to the temple and drives everyone from the area, both sheep and cattle; He scatters the coins of the money changers and overturns their tables. To those who sold doves He says, "'Get these out of here! How dare you turn my Father's house into a market!' His disciples remembered that it is written, 'Zeal for your house will consume me'" (John 2:13–17).

A messenger of God meets with John on an island one day when He is in the Spirit and among other things reveals to him a message for seven churches. One of these is a church in Laodicea. About this church Jesus says:

I know your deeds, that you are neither cold nor hot. I wish you were either one or the other! So, because you are luke-warm—neither hot nor cold—I am about to spit you out of my mouth. You say, "I am rich; I have acquired wealth and do not need a thing." But you do not realize that you are wretched, pitiful, poor, blind and naked. I counsel you to buy from me gold refined in the fire, so you can become rich; and white clothes to wear, so you can cover your shameful nakedness; and salve to put on your eyes, so you can see.

Those whom I love I rebuke and discipline. So be ear-nest, and repent. Here I am! I stand at the door and knock. If anyone hears my voice and opens the door, I will come in and eat with him, and he with me. (Rev. 3:15–20)

We need Him, and when we see He loves us enough to die for us, we love Him with all our heart, mind, strength and soul. And we need the Spirit to remind us.

His yoke is easy and His burden is light. From the beginning of the creation, God wanted humankind only to love Him, love each other and stay away from the knowledge of good AND evil. Pretty simple, right? That's easy submission, being tethered to the King of kings and the Lord of lords and the Spirit of God.

Submission by loving Him with all our strength, heart and mind. Being patriots for the cause, a living and speaking testi-mony of God's Grace. Zealots, hot for His house within us and for Him as Lord and Savior. A new identity. A new creation.

The yoke is easy and fastened with blessed assurance. We carry the simple burden of turning away from old thoughts about ourselves, fighting the tendencies within us and accepting the Spirit's power and renewal as we live out the remainder of our lives in transformative faith and a desire for God's presence.

People will see the evidence of the fiery work within us as the Spirit burns up the dross—the lies of bullies, identity killers, and our own multiple ways of falling short of our own perfection. We are changed, in a single moment by His grace—from worthless minions in a dead and broken world into beloved children of God. Beloved and valuable children of God!

As the Spirit's power changes us, we grow into our new identities and He shapes us into the likeness of Jesus! His presence also strengthens us with truth and redirection through grievous moments of discipline and training and into ministries of mercy and love in the world.

Those around us will see us as a new creation in our seemingly unexplained hope and in how we love them and how we love each other. They will see this in the way we praise and thank God and in our new attitudes toward them and how we live. They will see a passionate and zealous love for Jesus. They will see He's everything to us and will see us living as if we were saints who are seated in the heavenly realms (Eph. 1:20)—broken and imperfect, yet a grateful and gracious people.

We'll be watchful. We'll protect our homes, our families and our bodies from the dangers of being separated from God. We'll do this with a noble aim, an ambitious zeal. We'll do this because He first loved us from the cross, and we love Him now.

We'll live life in the Spirit and we'll find His love, joy and peace.

This Week

- Ask yourself if you need to study all the scriptures that refer to your new identity in Christ Jesus, if you need to meditate and increase your understanding of your new position as a child of God. Do you want to be strengthened in your inner being by this understanding?

- Ask the Lord if there's any rebellion in your life that He wants to reveal to you that you may submit it in repentance and prayer and be freed of its influence and its grieving upon His Spirit.

- Do you need prayers for your fervency toward the Lord, for your need and passion for Him, for your faith, that you may know you're filled with Him and walking with Him?

Please remember to do the following:

- Protect the life within you.
- Know who you are in Christ Jesus.
- Submit your desires to those of the Father.
- Be zealous for Him, for His house within your body wherever you go.

> "Here I am! I stand at the door and knock. If anyone hears my voice and opens the door, I will come in and eat with him, and he with me" (Rev. 3:20).

• • • •

coming into the beauty of His home . . .

Years ago, people were drawn from places far away to the little town out in the west. Many of them were artists looking to live among the beauty of the majestic red rocks, the sand and the desert plants. At night, the people of the town would often gather in a place high up where the stars and the moon made their home in the clear night. Some thought this place and others brought them the magic of being and a powerful current of life not found elsewhere. They shared crystals and special food to enrich their minds and to heighten the effect of their surroundings.

But, in their homes, in the privacy of their darkness, nothing changed in the broken vessels and bodies of clay they inhabited. Some were mean. Others were fearful and withdrawn and all sought to escape their fates within the crystalline sand they worshiped and were bound to . . . except for one, the one who found the first Artist waiting for him to come home, and into his workmanship and the good work He had for him.

O LORD, you are our Father.
We are the clay, you are the potter;
we are all the work of your hand.
(Is. 64:8)

10

THE BREATHTAKING MIRACLE OF BODY, SOUL AND SPIRIT

We love the streams in the mountains. Our family has spent many days enjoying quiet moments of reflection while listening to the steady sounds of water bubbling around rocks and moving through the trees and land around us. In the early years, our boys climbed the granite boulders standing in the flow. They fell into the streams and laughed as they felt their way through the wonder of polished stones and the crawly critters revealed beneath them.

Rivers run through life. They cut away at the banks as trees lean and then fall into them. Even the stones surrender their forms to the years of water pouring over them. Yet, they keep going just as we do. While the rivers remain, our spirits leave our well-lived bodies to continue into the next adventure.

> streams came up from the earth and watered the whole surface of the ground—the LORD God formed the man

from the dust of the ground and breathed into his nostrils
the breath of life, and the man became a living being.
(Gen. 2:6–7)

What a moment! Those in the heavens witness the breath-
taking miracle of new life and new human spirits in a world
created just for humankind.

He opens his eyes and he's alive. He can touch and see and
feel and hear the sounds of the streams cascading through
Eden. The sky is blue. The leaves are green. His Father is
there watching His son take his first steps and experiencing
the beauty all around him. From the dust, the body of Adam
rises, the one-of-a-kind, specially made man named Adam and
later the exquisitely made woman named Eve.

Adam is shaped from the clay of land and water and Eve is
made from a part of him. They both begin as bodies shaped
from the dust of the ground—innate material made of natural substances from the earth. The Creator, their Father,
then breathes into both of them a flowing spirit (*neshamah*)
capable of communing and relating to Him—a spiritual part
of their being.

They become living beings with a soul (*nephesh*)—a body
with a conscience, a willful strength, a depth of emotions,
a thoughtful mind, and the identity of an individual. Each a
special impression of their unique self: Adam and Eve.

The first man and woman didn't have a soul. They *were*
souls—distinct persons living on this earth made by God as
imagers of Him (in His image), little creators, and sons and
daughters of God. Their spirits made them alive to Him until

sin entered their lives and they were deadened by their trans-gressions (Eph. 2:1).

> May God himself, the God of peace, sanctify you through and through. May your whole spirit, soul and body be kept blameless at the coming of our Lord Jesus Christ. (1 Th. 5:23)

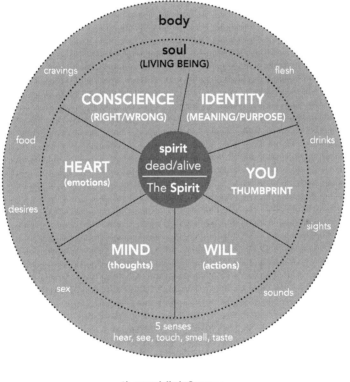

the world's influence
upon body, soul, spirit

For the word of God is living and active. Sharper than any double-edged sword, it penetrates even to dividing *soul and spirit*, joints and marrow; it judges the thoughts and attitudes of the heart. (Heb. 4:12)

You're First from the Dust of the Ground: Body and Soul

but streams came up from the earth and watered the whole surface of the ground—the Lord God formed the man from the dust of the ground. (Gen. 2:6–7)

It's interesting to see the symmetry of the Bible as a unified story that flows around and from its Author. Seventy-six percent of it is narrative and poetry poured into chapters and books and testaments about a singular quest. We see this as we read about its characters of kings and carpenters and supernatural forces. We feel and see the drama and struggle, the failures and victories. We feel them because they represent our own experiences.

Its big adventure and lost people tied together by a quest like that of the fellowship in Tolkien's *Lord of the Rings* stream around seen and unseen obstacles. They move through geography and time powered by an Author's love and pursuit of a happy ending. After thousands of passing years, it ends in peaceful and joyous resolution. John's prophecy describes the last days of the world's greatest narrative in this way:

Then the angel showed me the river of the water of life, as clear as crystal, flowing from the throne of God and of the Lamb down the middle of the great street of the city. On each side of the river stood the tree of life, bearing twelve crops of fruit, yielding its fruit every month. And the leaves of the tree are for the healing of the nations. No longer will there be any curse. The throne of God and of the Lamb will be in the city, and his servants will serve him. They will see his face, and his name will be on their foreheads. There will be no more night. They will not need the light of a lamp or the light of the sun, for the Lord God will give them light. And they will reign for ever and ever. (Rev. 22:1–5)

In the story's beginning, the waters are deep and formless and without light or life. Then streams burst forth and saturate the earth with the minerals and substances it needs to live and grow. It is at that moment that God chooses to form a man from the dust of the ground.

Like a master potter, God uses water to form two vessels from clay—man and woman. As He breathes into their bodies, the power of His Spirit turns them into living beings. They see, hear, smell, taste and feel the beauty of the garden. They are alive. They are conscious. They are His created beings. The story of humankind's rise and fall begins.

Scientists know that as much as 60 percent of a person's body is water. Ninety-nine percent of its mass contains oxygen, carbon, hydrogen, calcium and phosphorus. Each person begins as water and clay.

Every human being is a *nephesh*—a soul with a body that evaluates, experiences and acts upon the world around it. Some are artists or poets, singers or dancers. Others work the land and help it to produce. And the rest think about things, engineer them and keep them in a right and legal order or structure.

Some people have a deeper range of emotions and empathy. Those with a strong action orientation enjoy managing checklists and staying busy, while the more rational types like to analyze and understand the details and pieces of the objects in their care. As is obvious to the careful observer, God made our brains to work in different ways with various gifts and passions placed in us for the benefit of each other, the world around us and His glory.

In the beginning, all around and in us was very good. We loved each other with our unique differences as we tended and cared for the earth. We were naked and without shame. It was beautiful. It was paradise. It was perfection. It was amazing. It was thrilling. It was fun. It was thought-provoking. It was life. There are not enough adjectives in the human language to describe how it was or how it will be again.

God said, "It was good."

With a Wondrous Spirit Made to Enjoy Him

Flesh gives birth to flesh, but the Spirit gives birth to spirit. (John 3:6)

The Spirit gives life; the flesh counts for nothing. (John 6:63)

This is a mystery. Atheists and scientists debate but cannot solve it. People are more than clay—they are conscious.

People can know peace. They can know joy. They can know love. They can know sacrifice. There's something unique about each of them—something special, even in their fingerprints and their DNA. People are "spirit-ual."

God made us to walk and talk with Him and to enjoy this beautiful creation united with Him in our spirits (1 Cor. 6:17). Just as God is Spirit, we're each a spirit (like the other sons of God in the heavenly host) made in His likeness to be His image bearers in this world (Gen. 1:26–27). Because of the spirit within us, we were made from the beginning with the ability to spiritually discern the talk of God—the things that come from His Spirit. We were made to talk and walk with Him. We were made in His likeness.

John tells us that the words Jesus speaks and that we hear are spirit. They are also life. He came that we might have life (again) to the full (John 10:10).

Therefore, we worship Him in our spirit and in the truth of His words (John 4:24; 6:63). As Jesus explains His kingdom to a woman at a well, He uses water as a metaphor when He says, "Whoever believes in me, as the Scripture has said, streams of *living water* will flow from within him" (John 7:38). The apostle Paul, in his ministry to the Corinthians, later explains that the things that come from God are spiritually discerned (1 Cor. 2:14). We hear the things of God in our spirits from His Spirit.

The results of walking in the Spirit—love, joy, peace, patience, kindness, goodness faithfulness, gentleness and self-control—enter our lives. Born again, God makes us into a family unified in His love on earth. Adam and Even had no worries and only one concern—not to eat from a particular tree, one that would teach them good and evil and the spirit of independence and rebellion.

As they trusted Him, wanted Him and obeyed Him, life was full and their spirits were naturally ones of:

- love (Gal. 5:22; 2 Tim. 1:7)
- joy and rejoicing (Gal. 5:22; Luke 1:47)
- peace (Gal. 5:22)
- patience (Gal. 5:22)
- kindness Gal. 5:22)
- goodness (Gal. 5:22)
- faithfulness (Psa. 51:10; Gal. 5:22)
- gentleness 1Cor. 4:21; 1 Pet. 3:4
- self-control and discipline toward the things of God (Gal. 5:22; 2 Tim. 1:7)
- willingness (Psa. 51:12)
- power and strength (Luke 1:80; 2 Tim. 1:7)
- wisdom (Deut. 34:9)
- quietness (1 Pet. 3:4)
- unity (Rom. 15:5; Phil. 2:2)

What happened?

Your Dead Spirit Needs Him in You for a New Life

We left Him. We rebelled as did some of the heavenly host. Our spirits died as a result of our transgressions and sins. We forgot who we were and who made us. Our bodies chose what we wanted and what was offered in a land filled with the temptations of fallen sons of God. Out hearts filled with envy, covetous thoughts and pride. We hurt each other. We went to war. We gathered ourselves together with kings to lead us.

Prejudice and hate entered our souls. We were cut off from the words of God by our own fallen flesh and natural tendencies toward evil: "The Lord saw how great man's wickedness on the earth had become, and that every inclination of the thoughts of his heart was only evil all the time" (Gen. 6:5).

Today, without Him, without being born again, without His Spirit to strengthen us in our inner being, we have only the fallen sons of God and their created world systems and disorder to guide us. For example, people find their identities shaped by what they do, what they know or by what other people tell them. Ask a person, "Who are you?" and answers will range from words about their profession, their performance or their favorite ball team. They seek to find their identity and its self-esteem or self-worth in these—their intrinsic need for meaning or belonging. They walk around with spiritual amnesia and forget they're children of God: sons of the Most High!

When these fake identity markers fail them, which they do, they become anxious in their inner selves and without peace—depressed in their spirits. Parents push their children in the beginning of their fragile new lives to look and behave in a certain way in order to gain love and acceptance. They receive new names like fatty, stud, good-for-nothing, beauty queen, lazy and coward. Their worth is measured by different rulers, batting averages, job earnings, mirrors and the words of other lost people:

> "Mirror, mirror here I stand
> Who's the fairest the land?"
> (The evil queen, Wilhelm Karl Grimm, Grimm's Fairy Tale)

The inner voices screaming at them for attention result in hidden vows to never again be hurt. These drive them to fit in or compare what they do, or who they are, with others and lead to anorexic lives, bulimia and, in some people, suicide. Some just quit trying and sit in passive stupor as their damaged souls stop striving in the world.

Those who meet the world's demand for competence and "good looks" may never seem to feel like they measure up to an ever-moving mirage of acceptance and success. From another view, if their egos and self-promotion do inflate to see themselves as better and stronger than others, they lose empathy and a conscience for how they bring pain to and manipulate others. They become evil.

Today, sociopathic, psychotic and narcissist personalities are on the rise. The breakdown in the world's family, city and governmental cultures gives rise to thousands of hedonistic-focused people. Starting at an early age, they remove God from their lives, for some of these psychological states start when children seek to protect themselves from abuse, or their parents allow them to behave in any way that gets them what they want.

Even churches can become more secularized and focused on their own efforts and number and wealth. They stop talking about the movement and power of God. They stop loving Him. They stop testifying about Jesus on the doorposts of their homes and businesses. They quench and grieve the Spirit of God and turn from Him. Months pass without any significant evangelism or personal growth and sanctification. They lose any ambition to further the kingdom. They lose any ambition to continue their own spiritual growth and sanctification by the Spirit. Some even fall from grace.

The Transformation by the Spirit

> May God himself, the God of peace, sanctify you through and through. May your whole *spirit, soul and body* be kept blameless at the coming of our Lord Jesus Christ. (1 Th. 5:23)

We're a walking miracle—a remnant! The Spirit of God is within us! He's placed His temple in us! He's near. In His hand is the life (soul) of every creature and the breath (*ruah*, "spirit") of all humankind (Job 12:10). The Spirit brings life to our spirits. He's now our heart, our mind, our strength and our identity.

We watch and pray as we walk each day in the Spirit so that we don't fall into temptation. The spirit is willing, but the body, especially with years of old habits, is weak. As a new creation in Christ and a daily walk with Him, our lives become no longer "a matter of eating and drinking" and other desires of the flesh, "but of righteousness, peace and joy in the Holy Spirit" (Rom. 14:17).

That's because God has given us an undivided heart and a new spirit. He's removed our hearts of stone and given us hearts of flesh. As we read His words of truth and listen to Him throughout our days, He moves us to follow His decrees and keep His laws (Ezek. 36:26–27).

Jesus tells us that the Spirit gives life; the flesh counts for nothing. The words I have spoken to you are spirit and they are life (John 6:63). Please do nothing out of your own effort, thinking or emotions, but trust the Spirit to lead you as you pray and listen to Him and trust in His grace.

Five New Testament books end with the following:

- "May the *grace* of the Lord Jesus Christ, and the love of God, and the fellowship of the *Holy Spirit* be with you all" (2 Cor. 13:14).
- "The *grace* of our Lord Jesus Christ be with your *spirit*" (Gal. 6:18).
- "The *grace* of the Lord Jesus Christ be with your *spirit*" (Phil. 4:23).
- "The Lord be with your *spirit*. *Grace* be with you" (2 Tim. 4:22).
- "The *grace* of the Lord Jesus Christ be with your *spirit*" (Philem. 25).

And most of the rest of them end with "*grace* be with you."

This Week

- Ask yourself, "If you disagree with someone, are you both kind and direct?" By the way, do you know that many disagreements occur because people are different souls? Some feel deeper and express themselves with outward emotion. Others act with forceful quickness and confidence. Many are cautious and don't want to make mistakes. Our personalities are different and sometimes we don't appreciate the gifts of others. We so devalue them that we repel the gifted owner. This happens in a family, a business or a church body.

- What does the Spirit say to you from these verses? Job 17:1; Psa. 51:17; Is. 66:2; Matt. 5:3; Ezek. 11:19; 36:26; Rom. 8:9–15; 1 Cor. 2:10–14; Eph. 1:17; Job 32:8; Col. 2:13; Eph. 2:1, 5, 22; 1 John 4:13; Jude 19

  "I pray that out of his glorious riches he may strengthen you with power through his Spirit in your inner being" (Eph. 3:16). "I keep asking that the God of our Lord Jesus Christ, the glorious Father, may give you the Spirit of wisdom and revelation, so that you may know him better" (Eph. 1:17).

• • • •

gratitude when in the room . . .

I dreamed I was in a room with no windows or doors—no way out. I don't know how I got there, but there I was, alone and fearful. Sometimes I walked around and around feeling what I could feel of the walls and the floors, doing what I could do, seeing what I could see. Sometimes I was in pain and at other times felt a numbness in my predicament. I could hear people outside the room yet didn't want to call out, and much later sat in a corner by myself with the fear and pain.

I remembered a young child exploring the world around him with amazement and delight, a young woman in the first gasps of true love, a mother with her first child, a wiser bride beside her husband fighting for life, and a grandmother looking for help in the tiniest of needs.

Man or woman, young or old, we wear invisible chains, locked in rooms of all shapes and sizes, until it happens—the moment we cry out to Him. As we find ourselves sitting in the darkness and deepest gloom, He comes to us. He breaks our chains. And while in the room, even if we remain, we lift our voices in song, in gratitude, in praise. We are not the same. We are blessed by His presence. We're changed, no longer slaves to fear, but free.

Then they cried to the Lord in their trouble, and he saved them from their distress. He brought them out of darkness and the deepest gloom and broke away their chains.

Let them give thanks to the Lord for his unfailing love and his wonderful deeds for men. (Psa. 107:13–15)

11

EVIDENCE OF THE TRANSFORMED LIFE: THE FIRST MIRACLE

Is anyone the same after the Spirit draws that person to Jesus? Are you the same? Just as one hears the sound of the wind rushing through the trees or water trickling over rock in gentle urgency, you can also see the changed nature of a person being transformed and reborn in the Spirit of God. What begins with faith and the joy of accepting Him, ends in persevering seasons and moments of suffering, a yielded spirit and love.

Years before, when Clayton prayed before us or read Scripture from the Bible, people listened. This old sailor, who had served on warships, one day met Jesus and gave Him his life. Although not a practiced speaker, Clayton read the words he cherished with reverence and belief and a life changed through the ages by God. As I heard him and watched the power of gentleness and spiritual strength on display, my soul responded. Clayton is in some way a part of me today, the

Spirit working through him from past memories I have of him, influencing me during the last days of my life.

I remember the hospital room with his family pressed around him. They were singing hymns as the cancer was completing its work. A husband, a father to some, a grandfather to others, they all loved Clayton. I remember the room. I remember the soft sounds of singing around the bed. I remember his last words as he looked into their faces with a firm plea, "Be there!"

Some may finish like Clayton. Others may just be beginning, like my son Taylor.

Taylor's Story

"After 15 years of being trapped in the bottom of addiction's barrel, God pulled that stronghold off me. A few years ago, I would not have thought about giving God the credit for this. But looking back at the timeline of my failed attempts, I know that it was not of my own doing. I had tried getting rid of alcohol on my own for a decade; and in my last few years of drinking, I couldn't make it longer than a few days before the delirium tremors would be too much to handle and death from withdrawal was a true possibility. I was in a hell of my own making and powerless to stop it.

"One thing I did not expect is that it did not get any easier once the alcohol addiction had been removed. In fact, it became exponentially worse, and it stayed that way for a few years. I had become spiritually dead inside, and I was on the verge of my faith collapsing. My perception of the world and myself was bleak and miserable. I had horrific panic attacks, and even when those began to fade away, I felt like a bitter, empty shell of my former self.

"Sometimes, I doubted the existence of God. And if He did exist, I feared I would not measure up—that I would be turned away from His gates no matter how many times I genuinely repented. I prayed for forgiveness of the same things over and over again. No matter how many times I asked for it, I felt damned. I could stand outside on a perfect day and see no beauty. I was lost and despondent.

"Then, this thought started creeping into my head—that I should read all of the New Testament from Matthew to Revelation. I needed to discover if I still believed, because my faith was slipping away. Before reading each morning, I prayed for understanding and for God to show me what He wanted me to see. It was simple, and I meant it.

"When I read the following verses in Matthew, they were of particular importance to me:

"When an evil spirit comes out of a man, it goes through arid places seeking rest and does not find it. Then it says, 'I will return to the house I left.' When it arrives, it finds the house unoccupied, swept clean and put in order. Then it goes and takes with it seven other spirits more wicked than itself, and they go in and live there. And the final condition of that man is worse than the first. That is how it will be with this wicked generation." (Matt. 12:43–45)

"I truly believe that this occurred with me, and I can still see it clearly. After my personal demon of alcoholism was removed, I was sober, vulnerable, and an easy target. I had a host of darkness flood into me: self-hatred, depression, regret, doubt, anger, shame, despair, self-condemnation, hopelessness, etc. The list goes on and on. I was not expecting the weight of my past to be so condemning in my mind and heavy on my shoulders, and it was unrelenting for years.

"I began asking God to give me back what my soul had lost. I did not know what it was, but my joy in life was disappearing, and I desperately wanted it back. I prayed that he'd reignite the Holy Spirit's presence in me. I prayed to hear what was true and for guidance during my days. I prayed for his forgiveness. I prayed for him to change me.

"As I was reading the Gospel of Luke a couple of months later, I saw the New Covenant referenced in the footnotes. Now, my plan was to only read the New Testament. But I felt a pull to flip backwards, so I did.

> "The time is coming," declares the Lord, "when I will make a new covenant with the house of Israel and with the house of Judah. It will not be like the covenant I made with their forefathers when I took them by the hand to lead them out of Egypt, because they broke my covenant, though I was a husband to them,'"declares the Lord. "This is the covenant I will make with the house of Israel after that time," declares the Lord."I will put my law in their minds and write it on their hearts. I will be their God, and they will be my people. No longer will a man teach his neighbor, or a man his brother, saying, 'Know the Lord, 'because they will all know me, from the least of them to the greatest,"

declares the Lord. "For I will forgive their wickedness and will remember their sins no more." ." (Jer. 31:31–34)

"I could literally feel the weight lift off me and a warmth come over my soul. I felt what can only be described as a wave of deep, satisfying peace. The realization that in Jesus' sacrifice I have already been forgiven of my past became real. All of the self-hatred, depression, regret, doubt, shame, despair, self-condemnation, and hopelessness left me in the light of what they really were—false whispers in my ear and mind that were not from God.

"There it was right in front of me: 'I will forgive their wickedness and will remember their sins no more.'

"Since that inexplicable moment, I no longer feel guilty of my past. It was not a fleeting encounter, and the peace that I experienced in that room has not left me. In fact, I'm glad for what I have been through, because it's the path that has led me to a personal relationship with God and to a state where I can be present as a father to my son. I'm grateful for my sins having already been forgotten, and that gratefulness has only continued to grow. I feel alive again, and I will keep praying for guidance after being set free from severe, internal bondage.

"When I look back, I can see many of the things God was doing in my life while I was completely blind to them. I can see the hell I was in, and how he pulled me out of it. I can see how close I came to killing myself or someone else through extremely reckless actions, and I know I was spared consequences that would have been disastrous.

"My past no longer embarrasses me. The joy in life I once knew has been returning, and my self-loathing demons have been removed. My spirit is being restored, my faith is being renewed, and I can see more blessings in my life than I can count.

Miracle—A surprising and welcome event that is not explicable by natural or scientific laws and is therefore considered to be the work of a divine agency.

"We all have our own paths to walk, and our sins are unique to the personal choices we make. This is an attempt at putting into words my transformational experience that can only be explained in the Spirit.

"My morning prayers are simple, and reading the Bible has become my favorite part of the day. It lifts my spirit and fills me with hope. I can feel the Holy Spirit at work, and I can see the evidence of change in me that can only be divine in origin. If you're looking for something similar to happen in your own life, I can only point you directly to the source of miracles. May you find the waters of life and grow with Jesus in all of your days."

Remember this from Taylor's story: the way over the terrain may be difficult, the movement of the earth may throw you to your knees or smash your face to the ground, but you will rise even though weary. The Lord's hope placed firmly in you will help lift you to your feet. It will renew your strength and you will soar on wings like an eagle. You "will run and not grow weary, walk and not be faint" (Is. 40:31).

As a Christian, the Holy Spirit lives within you. He's the first miracle and evidence of a life in transformation.

Life is a disciplining path through the clutter and violent chaos of broken people and through a world at present orchestrated by unseen rulers. Yet, the kingdom of God advances through dead people brought to life by faith in Jesus—the born-again new creations who go among friends, family and neighbors with a testimony of words and love.

What Is Your New Name?

An uneducated fisherman casts a net into the lake. He does not have in his mind the things of God, but the things of men. His overly self-confident attitude displays itself in words and brash movements without wisdom. He acts bravely and boldly like many emotional young men often do, but when reality faces them, when spiritual courage is required, they lose their manhood. They deny. They look the other way. Such was Simon, in the beginning, when he met Jesus and later admitted, "Go away from me, Lord; I am a sinful man!" (Luke 5:8).

Simon is a soul with an unbridled heart and assertive manners. His early faith in Jesus as the Christ, the Son of the living God, is that of a heart caught up in adoration (Matt. 16:16). Although the Spirit is near him, He is not yet in Simon, whose excitable personality and faith are untethered at times. Jesus takes him and the other disciples onto a mountain to pray, and Moses and Elijah appear in splendor talking with Jesus, whose clothes become as bright as a flash of lightning. When Peter sees them about to leave, he tells Jesus, "Master, it is good for us to be here. Let us put up three shelters—one for you, one for Moses and one for Elijah" (Luke 9:29–33). (He does not know what he is saying.)

Simon also questions Jesus about His parables. He walks on water trying to follow Him. He takes Jesus aside to rebuke Him when He speaks of His death to come (Mark 8:33); and then just before Jesus' capture and subsequent crucifixion, he tells Him, "Even if I have to die with you, I will never disown you" (Mark 14:31). When the soldiers take Jesus, Simon denies Him three times.

Yet, Jesus sees the good to come in Simon—what the Spirit will do in and with him. Jesus knows who he'll become, and so names him Peter, which in Greek means "rock": "And I tell you that you are Peter and on this rock I will build my church, and the gates of Hades will not overcome it" (Matt. 16:18).

The Spirit is poured onto Peter on the day of Pentecost and this uneducated and often melodramatic fisherman leads the newly formed church in its first days. His inner spirit, now reborn and empowered by the Spirt of God, begins to direct his soul as a new being in Christ. On that day, a crowd forms in bewilderment when the Spirit of God like the sound of a violent wind fills the house and the disciples as they are praying. Peter begins to speak to them about Jesus, and when he finishes pleading with them and warning them with "many words," three thousand believe (Acts 2:41).

Several days later, after healing a beggar who had been crippled from birth, Peter speaks to a crowd of people who gather at the news. Many who hear his message believe and the number of new believers grows to five thousand. These conversions and Peter's testimony of Jesus attract the attention of priests, the captain of the temple guard and the Sadducees (they don't believe in spirits or angels or the resurrection, Acts 2:8).

The rulers, elders and teachers have Peter and John put in jail and brought to them the next day for questioning. They ask, "By what power or what name did you do this?" (Acts 4:7). Peter, filled with the Holy Spirit, gives a courageous response. When they hear Peter and John both reply, and realize they are unschooled, ordinary men, they are astonished and notice that these men have been with Jesus. After threatening them, the rulers command them to stop speaking in the name of Jesus, Peter replies, "we cannot help speaking about what we have seen and heard" (Acts 4:20).

Is this Simon? No! This is Peter, the rock—a new person in Christ now living life filled with the Spirit of God. Just like Clayton was no longer the boy who was a sailor, Peter is no longer the boy, Simon, the untethered fisherman. He is now a son of God and the Spirit fills him.

What is your name now that Jesus fills your heart? How is He taking your previously uncontrollable emotions, critical heart, your fearful timidity or pushy, ego-driven life and changed you? What do those around you say? Do they see the evidence of transformation, the miracle of a new creation?

When He fills you with His Spirit, you begin to change and become like Jesus. A spiritual transformation begins in you; and, unless you quench Him with your rebellion, or resist His grace for you, or lose your love for Him, you bring His peace and strength and encouragement and comfort to those who meet you. "For flesh gives birth to flesh, but the Spirit gives birth to spirit" (John 3:6).

As the years pass, the Spirit of God disciplines and changes us into loving and useful people who advance His kingdom. This does not always feel good but always ends in righteousness and peace when we allow His work in us.

Moreover, we have all had human fathers who disciplined us and we respected them for it. How much more should we submit to the Father of our spirits and live! Our fathers disciplined us for a little while as they thought best; but God disciplines us for our good, that we may share in his holiness. No discipline seems pleasant at the time, but painful. Later on, however, it produces a harvest of righteousness and peace for those who have been trained by it. (Heb. 12:9–11)

Not only so, but we also rejoice in our sufferings, because we know that suffering produces perseverance; perseverance, character; and character, hope. And hope does not disappoint us, because God has poured out his love into our hearts by the Holy Spirit, whom he has given us. (Rom 5:3–5)

Consider it pure joy, my brothers [and sisters], whenever you face trials of many kinds, because you know that the testing of your faith develops perseverance. Perseverance must finish its work so that you may be mature and complete, not lacking anything. (Jas 1:2–4)

We No Longer Fear: We Love as We Are Loved!

When my wife, Sheila, and I watch Zach Williams live from Harding Prison, we find ourselves encouraged by the song lyrics he sings and the heartfelt response of the prisoners. They help us remember who we are in Christ Jesus. The apostle Paul reminds us as well . . .

> For we know that our old self was crucified with him so that the body of sin might be done away with, that we should no longer be slaves to sin— because anyone who has died has been set free from sin.
>
> Now if we died with Christ, we believe that we will also live with him . . .
>
> You have been set free from sin and have become slaves to righteousness . . .
>
> For you did not receive a spirit that makes you a slave again to fear, but you received the Spirit of sonship. And by him we cry, "Abba, Father." (Rom. 6:6–8,18; 8:15)

People without Jesus or who live life alone in their own effort experience fears of being alone, loss, condemnation, failure, success, being unlovable, losing control, being wrong, oppression or death. Their fears cause them to live in self-made prisons of anxiety, depression, anger or passive loneliness. We need to remember the words of Paul when these fears occur. Also, we can meditate on and remember what he told Timothy, "For God did not give us a spirit of timidity [fear], but a spirit of power, of love and of self-discipline" (2 Tim. 1:7).

In August 2016, the Gospel Music Association (GMA) nominated "No Longer Slaves" for a Dove Award in the "Worship Song of the Year" category. On October 11, 2016, the song won the GMA Dove Award at a ceremony held at the Allen Arena on the campus of Lipscomb University in Nashville, Tennessee, with Jonathan David and Melissa Helser performing the song that night. Millions upon millions have heard this song and it touches the fears of their hearts. (Jonathan's and Melissa's testimony is here: https://youtu.be/cWl6lhodTMI)

The Zach Williams video cover tribute shown on YouTube and performed at Harding Prison has had 36 million views as of December, 2020. Why? Because the lyrics touch a part of us that wants freedom from the bondage of sin and a life lived in our own effort. In the tribute, we see men in a prison worshiping God and calling on His name.

The words of this song explain that children of God have been freed from fear. They are no longer slaves to it. They have been lifted out of a past life of sin and placed in the arms of God. They are chosen. They are born again. And they are accepted into a new family with a Father who surrounds them with love.

It's a song of deliverance.
It's a song of perfect love.
It's a song of freedom.
It's a song for sons and daughters of God.

God knows your name. He wants you to be His child. He wants you to know His son. He wants you to respond to the story of Jesus you find in a song, in a poem, in a story, or in the testimony of someone you meet. The message of faith, hope and love is found in "No Longer Slaves," and prisoners singing at Harding Prison. The words encourage us to leave a life of fearful bondage in our own efforts and to live free in the Spirit of God.

The grace of the Lord Jesus Christ is a miracle! His Spirit in us is a miracle! As new creations in Christ Jesus, we're a born-again, born-from-above miracle! Jesus tells us, "So if the Son sets you free, you will be free indeed" (John 8:36).

Go and light up the world as God sings over you: "The LORD your God is with you, he is mighty to save. He will take great delight in you, he will quiet you with his love, he will rejoice over you with singing" (Zeph. 3:17). Hallelujah! Go JESUS!

This Week

- An interesting exercise ... You were born with a name given to you by your parents before you knew Christ Jesus and before the Spirit began your transformation. If He gave Simon the name Peter and we then see this brash and emotional young man becoming the "Rock" of the early church, what name would describe you now as a new creation in Christ. What name would describe your character and personality now versus yesterday?

  Clayton and Simon and Saul grew over a lifetime of surrender to the Spirit of God. They all finished well, different, better and more like Jesus.

  So will you.

- Do you relate at all to this? "People without Jesus or who live life alone in their own effort live with a fear of being alone, loss, condemnation, failure, success, being unlovable, losing control, being wrong, oppression, or death."

  Their fears cause them to live in self-made prisons of anxiety, depression, anger or passive and lonely imprisonment. Confess any of these (or fears I've not mentioned) to the Lord and ask for the Spirit to set you free from them. Meditate on any of the words of God in this chapter and remember, God did not give you "a spirit of timidity [fear], but a spirit of power, of love and of self-discipline" (2 Tim. 1:7).

· You're being transformed into the likeness of Christ Jesus every day as His ambassador. Don't quench the Spirit or grieve Him by going off in your own effort. Ask him to fill you each day as you start and end the day with praise and thanksgiving.

> "Him who overcomes I will make a pillar in the temple of my God. Never again will he leave it. I will write on him the name of my God and the name of the city of my God, the new Jerusalem, which is coming down out of heaven from my God; and I will also write on him my *new name* (Rev. 3:12)."

. . . .

our sacred houses . . .

It's early morning and a business man rises with thoughts of the day ahead as he shaves and puts on his best. Walking through his home and past his wife and children, he grabs his coffee and hurriedly moves to his car and the road. During his journey, the traffic flashes past him before he slows down and eases into his parking space. Getting out of his car, he walks to his office. He begins the day before the others and prepares himself for what he must do. The hours fly by into the afternoon and to the time of his departure back to his home and along the same roads. When he arrives, the house is empty—everyone is gone. The money is gone, the furniture is gone, the grass and trees have covered the flowers of the past. He looks inside himself and finds it empty there as well—no one to strengthen, to encourage, to comfort.

The Spirit lives within some of us—His temple is in our house—the one we carry with us. He's in our homes and cars and offices as well. He's in the countryside and in the cities and in our sports and hobbies. Everywhere we look and take ourselves, He goes with us and is in us. Our many houses will be houses of prayer—our spirits with His Spirit—and in all of our days we'll be like trees planted by the rivers of water, in our going in and in our going out, we'll walk with Him. He'll be with us. He'll keep us safe.

But I tell you the truth: It is for your good that I am going away. Unless I go away, the Counselor will not come to you; but if I go, I will send him to you.. (John 16:7)

It is written, "My house will be a house of prayer." (Matt. 21:13; Mark 11:17; Luke 19:46)

12

PRAY IN THE SPIRIT OF GOD

Years ago, a familiar phrase was often heard on television and in the movies. A mom would say as she tucked her child into bed for a good night's sleep, "Now John, be sure and say your prayers!" On some Hallmark channels, this sweet cliché still occurs. What about your home? Is your home a house of prayer?

Matthew, Mark, Luke and John all record a fiery aggression in our Lord's life. He's consumed by zeal for the temple of God when He sees money changers and merchants buying and selling there. With forceful intent he makes a whip out of cords. He then enters the temple area and overturns their tables and benches and drives out the sheep, cattle and people. As He does, He exclaims, "Get these out of here! How dare you turn my Father's house into a market!" ... "It is written," he said to them, "'My house will be a house of prayer'; but you have made it 'a den of robbers.'" (John 2:13–17; Luke 19:46)

Interestingly, the word "house" appears in many forms in the Bible:

- The house within you; God's new temple is in you.
- The house of your family; like the house of David, of Saul, of the Coopers'.
- The house of God; the body of believers; multiple temples in present times.
- The house of our country; like the house of Israel, the nation, the USA.

You are now God's temple and the Spirit of God lives in you. His temple is sacred and you are that temple. You are not your own (1 Cor. 3:16–17; 6:19). His divine presence is within you. When you don't walk in your own effort but with His Spirit, you affect everyone around you with His power. You change the world.

This means that wherever we go, whatever we do, we carry with us the Spirit of God and pray in the Spirit on all occasions (Eph. 6:18). Our bodies are houses of prayer. Our homes are houses of prayer. Our lineages, if full of faithful people, are houses of prayer. The place we gather with other believers are houses of prayer first, not singing, not studying, not places of hearing sermons, not places of service, but houses of prayer first and always in the Spirit.

Praying in the Spirit

Our prayers are like memorial offerings to God—like golden bowls full of incense, the prayers of all the saints going up before God. The prayers of His children are precious to Him. They show an important depth of faith, belief and trust in Him and not in ourselves (Acts 10:4, Rev. 5:8; 8:3–4).

While writing this book, my study has led me to many scriptural examples of being full of the Spirit, walking in the Spirit and praying in the Spirit. In this time of reading and prayer, I have become aware of a life with God that is deeper and wider than I had previously understood.

Important questions have occurred to me. How many times have I walked through days and crucial moments without prayer? Was I doing most things with my own effort? What about when I developed and taught the series of lessons in this book? Was I continually being filled with the Spirit? What does that even mean? How will my prayer life change? What did the disciples see in His posture or His attitude, when Jesus began to pray, "Our Father who art in heaven, hallowed be thy name" (Matt. 6:9)?

My journey became intellectually and emotionally overwhelming about three weeks before I wrote these words. After listening to many voices and reading Scripture for hours, I was sitting in my car, in the parking lot at the Loudon County Cooperative. Farmers were driving up. There were bags of feed and other farming materials to buy near the door. I sat there and felt the need to call Harlan, one of my best friends in this life with Jesus.

After discussing what I was learning, I told him, "For some reason, I'm scared of what asking God to fill me with His Spirit means. It's like facing the unknown. It's like major submission—humility—trust in Him. It's more than illogical, or raw emotion or unrestrained willpower. It's not knowing what 'in His Spirit' really means. Very few people seem to know around me."

Harlan, sensing something at a deeper level, said, "Let's pray."

Right there, in my truck, at the Cooperative, we did. It turned out to be the perfect thing to do at that time—to pray in the Spirit without any idea about what to pray for, to just give it to God. I think most of life requires this type of prayer.

Since then nothing strange or extra-marvelous has occurred, but I'm continuing to search the Scriptures. I do find myself praying more often during the day and when I go to bed and wake up at night. I'm praying for the saints, for all of those I know, by name each day.

- *Live* by the Spirit (Gal. 5:25).
- *Worship* in the Spirit (John 4:24).
- *Pray* in the Spirit . . . in the Holy Spirit (Eph. 6:18; Jude 20).

> And pray in the Spirit on all occasions with all kinds of prayers and requests. With this in mind, be alert and always keep on praying for all the saints. (Eph. 6:18)

As the kingdom of God spread among the cities, a church was established in the town of Ephesus. In Paul's letter to the Christians there, he begins with the mystery of God's will. He tells them that when the times have reached their fulfillment all things in heaven and on earth will come together under one authority—Jesus. All believers will be with Him, redeemed in Him and marked with a seal—the promised Holy Spirit.

Paul writes that he's heard about their faith in Jesus and their love for all the saints. He tells them that he continues to give thanks for them and that he remembers them in his prayers. He wants them to know that Jesus has an incomparably great power for them as believers—one that is greater than that of all rulers, authorities, and powers of this dark world—a power within them that will protect them from the spiritual forces of evil in the heavenly realms (Eph. 1:19; 6:12).

With a profound humility and posture before God, do you pray in the Spirit on all occasions and for all the saints around you? Do you pray for those you don't like? Do you pray for your leaders who stand on the front lines nearest to demonic forces of evil? Do you pray for those who testify and preach the gospel, that when they open their mouths, words may be given to them that they will fearlessly make known the mystery of the gospel (Eph. 6:19)? Do you pray for the ministries of the saints around you? Do you pray in the Spirit as a dwelling in which God lives, or do you pray in your own effort, and mostly for yourself? I'm learning to pray for all the saints—for each of you when I go to sleep and when I awake in the night.

> For this reason I kneel before the Father, from whom his whole family in heaven and on earth derives its name. I pray that out of his glorious riches he may strengthen you with power through his Spirit in your inner being, so that Christ may dwell in your hearts through faith. And I pray that you, being rooted and established in love, may have

power, together with all the saints, to grasp how wide
and long and high and deep is the love of Christ, and to
know this love that surpasses knowledge—that you may
be filled to the measure of all the fullness of God.

Now to him who is able to do immeasurably more than
all we ask or imagine, according to his power that is at
work within us, to him be glory in the church and in Christ
Jesus throughout all generations, for ever and ever! Amen.
(Eph. 3:14–21)

Paul prays this prayer while he suffers in chains, in prison,
in the dark. He's in prison yet we hear confidence and freedom. This is a prayer in the Spirit. Do we want to pray in the
Spirit? At this depth?

Recently, Sheila, my wife, lost her mom. She was like a
second mother to me. Alice, at 95, died of COVID as she was
rehabilitating from surgery. This occurred a few miles from
an assisted living facility in which just a year previous she had
attended dancing and fencing classes.

In the days after, Sheila realized her mom was more a part
of her than she was ready to understand or face. When I asked
her to reflect on this time, she said, "It was like I didn't know
who I was anymore. So much of who I was, was caught up in
the relationship and the family my mom loved. I felt a part of
me had died and I wasn't the same person. It was like a part
of my heart had been ripped out. The only thing that gave me
peace was knowing that He is God."

Sheila explained that during the ensuing days, she walked
among the trees, "Just crying out and in communion with

Him. I realized that praising Him got me through the day as I remembered her and thanked Him over and over. It was like I lost purpose or didn't care anymore. I didn't enjoy doing the things I loved. I didn't want to do them anymore—a depressed spirit perhaps. Even the everyday tasks and the routines of life, previously my joy with God, were blocked."

I thank my amazing lady in Christ Jesus for sharing her heart. It was painful for her to remember, yet now no longer a burden of pain to hold her back. Even though the hurt resurfaces at times, she receives God's peace as He gives her power over it.

Hannah's story is written in the first book of Samuel. Her heart cries out over her barren and childless existence as a woman. Though loved by her husband, year after year she is provoked and irritated by a rival over her inability to have children. This happens even when she goes to worship at the house of the Lord. It occurs so frequently that she will not eat and appears downcast when she is with her husband.

This emotional turmoil continues to dominate her life until one day, in bitterness of soul Hannah weeps much and prays to the Lord:

> As she kept on praying to the LORD, Eli observed her mouth. *Hannah was praying in her heart, and her lips were moving* but *her voice was not heard.* Eli thought she was drunk and said to her, "How long will you keep on getting drunk? Get rid of your wine."
>
> "Not so, my lord," Hannah replied, "I am a woman who is deeply troubled. I have not been drinking wine or beer;

I was pouring out my soul to the LORD. Do not take your servant for a wicked woman; I have been praying here out of my great anguish and grief."

Eli answered, "Go in peace, and may the God of Israel grant you what you have asked of him."

She said, "May your servant find favor in your eyes." Then she went her way and ate something, and her face was no longer downcast. (1 Sam. 1:12–18)

Sheila, in remembering the story, said, "Hanna was so distraught and desirous of having a child. That experience of emotional loss was happening to me with Mom. It was a surprise because I knew she was ready to go to Jesus, but the pain afterwards was a shock. I think this occurred because of the depth of my connection with her that up until then I did not understand."

Sheila's and Hannah's prayers were prayed in humility and anguish in the Spirit. They were both helpless to do anything to change the hurt of their circumstances. Sheila said, "I knew that I could not do anything under my own power to heal." (If you want to listen to Sheila's story and her walk in the Spirit, please use this link: https://tinyurl.com/yxlgkopq)

Praying in the Spirit means to give up the past, present and future. It's the picture of a child hidden in the protective arms of a father when things are good or bad. It is receiving strength and healing in submission to His power and love. It is yielding everything to His perfect control of our lives. We die to ourselves in Him with thanksgiving, praise and prayers for all the saints. We pray for His kingdom to come! "But you, dear friends, build yourselves up in your most holy faith and pray in the Holy Spirit" (Jude 20).

And pray in the Spirit on all occasions with all kinds of prayers and requests. With this in mind, be alert and always keep on praying for all the saints. (Eph. 6:18)

And when you stand praying, if you hold anything against anyone, you will forgive that person, so that your Father in heaven may forgive you your sins. (Mark 11:25).

I thank my God every time I remember you. In all my prayers for all of you, I always pray with joy. (Phil. 1:3–4)

You learned it from Epaphras, our dear fellow servant, who is a faithful minister of Christ on our behalf, and who also told us of your love in the Spirit. For this reason, since the day we heard about you, we have not stopped praying for you and asking God to fill you with the knowledge of his will through all spiritual wisdom and understanding. (Col. 1:7–9)

Devote yourselves to prayer, being watchful and thankful. And pray for us, too, that God may open a door for our message, so that we may proclaim the mystery of Christ, for which I am in chains. Pray that I may proclaim it clearly, as I should. (Col. 4:2–4)

This Week

- Pray in the Spirit on all occasions with all kinds of prayers and requests. With this in mind, be alert and always keep on praying for all the saints. Do this by name if possible for those you know and then for the Christ believers throughout the world.

- Especially do this for those with whom you have had disagreements or for those you need to forgive. Tell God about how you were hurt, how it felt and ask Him to heal you of the pain and any remaining malice toward those who harmed you. Let go and pray for blessings in their lives through His power within you.

- When the Spirit prompts you, pray with and for someone. When by yourself, pray, "Your kingdom come, your will be done on earth as it is in heaven" (Matt. 6:10) Pray with your hands raised or your head bowed in submission. Pray to Him. Sing to Him. Ask Him for your daily bread. "Delight yourself in the Lord and He will give you the desires of your heart" (Psa. 37:4). He'll put desires within you through His Spirit and will give you only the ones that will be good for you.

- Life is complex. People are complex. The war in the heavens and on earth is complex. Give up and submit. Die to yourself until only Christ lives in you and your prayers and discussions with Him will be real and pleasing to Him as His child.

· Our houses will be houses of prayer, so let's build ourselves up in our most holy faith and pray in the Holy Spirit on all occasions with all kinds of prayers and requests. With this in mind, let's be alert and always praying for all the saints (John 2:13–17; Eph. 6:18; Jude 19–20).

• • • •

the work that counts . . .

*It flew through the old log house and into a great
room of beams and rafters. Their cat watched it
intently, looking for the moment when it swept
toward the ground. The family called to each other
and pointed out the dilemma—a beautiful gift of God
trapped in a place of harm. With the Spirit guiding
them, they knew to work to free the bird as they
followed its flight and found the way to guide it out of
an open window and into the outside light.*

*Birds are preyed upon by man and beast. The snares
are set. The traps are laid. In this place, the Spirit
gives each of us our work of production, protection
and provision for those He brings our way. When
we walk with Him, He takes away our anxieties for
food or clothing or money and uses us to advance
His kingdom into the hearts of those in trouble.
His Spirit does His work through us with a word
or something from Him that brings them to Jesus.
As new creations, they make it to the open window
and to freedom as He brings them into the light. We
continue to feed them on the journey as we work and
learn and grow together.*

Look at the birds of the air; they do not sow or reap or store away in barns, and yet your heavenly Father feeds them. (Matt. 6:26)

Jesus said, "Feed my sheep." (John 21:18)

13

SPIRITUAL WORK THAT WILL MAKE US LIKE JESUS

What would it have been like to eject from your plane into North Vietnamese territory during the Vietnam War? What if you were the pilot they would parade in front of cameras as a trophy for their propaganda? Would you beat your face with a wooden stool? Would you cut your own scalp with a razor just to keep from being a pawn of humiliation for your country and your fellow prisoners?

Admiral James Stockdale, Medal of Honor recipient, did this and many other heroic actions during his seven-and-a-half years of imprisonment at the "Hanoi Hilton." Later, in his business book *Good to Great*, the author Jim Collins, using a rule called the "Stockdale Paradox," described the admiral's disciplined effort to survive: "You must never confuse faith that you will prevail in the end . . . with the discipline to confront the most brutal facts of your current reality" (Collins,

J. C. (2001). Good to Great: Why Some Companies Make the Leap... and Others Don't. HarperBusiness).

James, the brother of Jesus, shares a gospel spiritual law in much the same way:

> Consider it pure joy, my brothers, whenever you face trials of many kinds, because you know that *the testing of your faith develops perseverance.* Perseverance must finish its work so that you may be mature and complete, not lacking anything. If any of you lacks wisdom, he should ask God, who gives generously to all without finding fault, and it will be given to him. But when he asks, he must believe and not doubt, because he who doubts is like a wave of the sea, blown and tossed by the wind . . .
>
> *Blessed is the man who perseveres under trial, because when he has stood the test,* he will receive the crown of life that God has promised to those who love him. (Jas 1:2–6, 12)

The good news does not always feel "good," but it *is* good. Joy is a spiritual blessing of the Spirit and is separate from a person's feelings. The Greek word in this passage, derived from the verb *chairō* for "rejoice" or "be glad," conveys a joy rooted in spiritual union and is related to why we were put in Eden ("The Lord God took the man and put him in the Garden of Eden to work it and take care of it." [Gen. 2:15]). In the beginning, humankind lived as God's children walking with Him, working the land while secure in His presence and love.

Joy was a natural part of being in union with Him and each other doing our parts in the world He created for us.

Now, we return to Him through our faith in Jesus. He lives inside us. Safe within God's family, we face the trials of working in a broken world while always connected by the Spirit in the kingdom of God. The root of the word "joy" implies a charisma, or "a special magnetic charm or appeal", a joy that arises from what we do for Him. It represents a spiritual gifting of joy from our perseverance when tested. It occurs in us while we farm the land and tend and take care of what we've been given; even as we continue to spread His love and good news during storms, droughts, and the pain of life.

Joy, then, is like a mountain spring that bubbles up from the ground pure. It's like a stream of living water that escapes as a product of all the other fruit of the Spirit—love, peace, patience, kindness, goodness, faithfulness, gentleness and self-control. It refreshes our souls on all occasions. It is not dependent upon circumstances. It is a gift of faith working within and against the elements of this world as together we advance the kingdom of God with force.

Knowing we're secure within God's family, we do His will on earth. Rejoicing rises as we work filled with and dependent upon the Spirit of God. Joy bubbles up from the Spirit's effervescent combination of faith and work—a gifting of joy to each person. Joy, then, occurs in our darkest moments and in our best ones and in all the days of our new life as new creations at work. In 1874, Knowles Shaw, inspired by Psalm 126:6, captured our rejoicing in every moment with the lyrics to "Bringing in the Sheaves"—working without fear, laboring, weeping, in sunshine and in winter, sowing for the Master, bringing in the sheaves:

> Sowing in the morning, sowing seeds of kindness,
> Sowing in the noontide and the dewy eve;
> Waiting for the harvest, and the time of reaping,
> We shall come rejoicing, bringing in the sheaves.
>
> Bringing in the sheaves, bringing in the sheaves,
> We shall come rejoicing, bringing in the sheaves,
> Bringing in the sheaves, bringing in the sheaves,
> We shall come rejoicing, bringing in the sheaves.
>
> Sowing in the sunshine, sowing in the shadows,
> Fearing neither clouds nor winter's chilling breeze;
> By and by the harvest, and the labor ended,
> We shall come rejoicing, bringing in the sheaves.
>
> Going forth with weeping, sowing for the Master,
> Though the loss sustained our spirit often grieves;
> When our weeping's over, He will bid us welcome,
> We shall come rejoicing, bringing in the sheaves.

The Work That Harms Us

Paul tells us that "the only thing that counts is *faith expressing itself in love*" (Gal. 5:6). And, James tells us, "*Do not merely listen to the word*, and so deceive yourselves. Do what it says." Faith and actions work together. He promises us that "in the doing," we'll be blessed in what we do (Jas 1:22, 25; 2:22).

But how do we know what to do and how much of and when and where to do it? There are many ways to love God and others and for our faith to be expressed. How can we ever be right with God? How can we make sure we do enough?

We could start with the Ten Commandments or, better still, read the Bible and compile a list of all the commands we can find. When we hear teaching that reveals some we missed, we could add to the list. We could do this in a Google spreadsheet or in a simple notebook.

But here's the problem: we'll still fall short. How would we use social media, or how many people would we pray for, or how long should we pray and for what things, when? What would we wear or not wear? Who would we listen to? (I think we would stop listening, because that would mean we would have to add more activities to the list.)

To steward our bodies, what would we eat and not eat and in what quantities? What about exercise? What about our entertainment? Would we watch television? How much? How often? What shows would we avoid? Whom would we vote for? In what ways would we love our spouse or our children? When? How much sacrifice would be required within how many hours of the day?

You get the point. Living like this would be like existing in prison—a prison of impossible perfection. It would be a life without the Spirit of God and without His work in us; and, eventually we would look judgmentally upon ourselves and upon others. We might become spiritual sociopaths controlling the world around us or guilt-laden people running from religion's no-mercy rule.

Satan stirs up this kind of mess inside the children of God with lies about the grace of God. He uses the world's demand for competence and various measuring sticks. We do a good job of this too as we try to reach our own goals with our human effort and without the Spirit. I can look back at many days and see not only my failures and lack of spiritual maturity, but also the anxiety within me from either my sinful condition or my internal struggle with judgment.

Either through obvious sin or the private curtain of hidden sin, in seeking to control our circumstances, we work to please ourselves by fulfilling our own desires. We strike the rock to drink our own way and lose the Spirit's living water flowing from within. In this state, God knows we love neither him nor others. Our hearts are far from Him. We don't have a relationship with Him based on love, trust and grace. We don't seek His presence or counsel. We don't know Him. We're off on our own.

To leave this body of death, we reach a point of decision: to continue drowning in deadly pools of dark waters, or to leave behind God and this earth through suicide—or to die to ourselves and live for Christ.

Lift your arms to God. Kneel before Him. Trust in the Lord with all your heart. Acknowledge Him in all your ways and He'll direct your paths. He is Lord of lords, King of kings and the God of all creation. He is both the Lamb and the Lion of Judah. *He is!* . . . (When Sheila walked in her home or in the forest as she sought God amidst her pain from the loss of her mom, she prayed and played "He is [the names of God] [Return of Majesty Trilogy][https://youtu.be/NscHCa395-M]" over and over and over as her spirit sought His healing and perfect voice. She needed to know He is!)

The Spiritual Work That Transforms Us

When we change masters, we change the type of work and the way we go about it. Some leaders make their cultures ones of control and fear and power. Others make them soft and weak and passive. The kingdom of God is led by the Spirit and the grace of God and unimaginable power. We're the noble patriots of a heavenly cause and an ambitious plan. Our Master and Lord is Jesus!

We work to advance His rule on earth within the hearts of people. We labor together in the Spirit. We know that Jesus has set us free from slavery to sin and fear. We respond to Him with gratefulness and sacrifice and obedience. In difficult circumstances, those around us see our love, joy, peace, patience, kindness, gentleness, faithfulness, goodness, and self-control.

I believe that praying in the Spirit begins our journey of faith and transformation as Jesus uses us as His ambassadors. We do this "for the sake of the gospel"—the good news, and to "share in its blessings" (1 Cor. 9:23; 2 Cor. 5:20). As children of God, we love Him with our heart, mind and strength. In differing amounts and in different times and seasons. And with the Spirit directing us, we repent of sin, meditate on His word, reset our minds, fast in His presence, minister in the fields.

God chases you to save and bring you back to Him. It's His story of love. He did this for me. He'll do it for you. The Spirit of God drew me to Him at 16 years of age. I remember being drawn to the grace of God and His son Jesus. As the

Spirit brought me to my feet to confess His name to those in my church, I remember turning to my friend next to me and saying, "Keith, let's go!" He shook His head, "No." At that moment, I thought those around me were compelled to go as well.

In faith and with the Spirit's leading, I entered the waters of baptism. I emerged a new creation. Much work remained to be done in the years ahead. Parts of me the Spirit disciplined and brought under His control, but the war waged on from within and from without.

When I was in my thirties, my sins brought me to a moment in my life where we were about to lose our home through my laziness, my immaturity, my anger toward my dad, my sins—all my days controlled by me. The complexities of a life lived on my terms forced me to my knees at 2:00 a.m. My wife and children asleep, I died to myself, gave Christ my life, and told Him it was His. I surrendered with my head on the floor and asked Him to just "Please let me keep my family." With this confession, Jesus touched me again and my repentance began anew . . .

Falling asleep in peace, I later awoke with the circumstances the same. But I was different. Satan's hold on me had been broken. I was free, but work remained.

After years of reading motivational books and listening to self-help gurus, I replaced all of them with the Bible. I spent hours alone and deep into many nights led by the Spirit to read and, using a typewriter, type out the scriptures He knew I needed. The Spirit led me to those I needed for my growth—those He knew would be personal to me and for me.

I meditated on and memorized some of special importance. Here's one: "The LORD is my strength and my shield; my heart trusts in him, and I am helped. My heart leaps for joy and I will give thanks to him in song." (Psa. 28:7). And another: "Trust in the LORD with all your heart and lean not on your own understanding; in all your ways acknowledge him, and he will make your paths straight." (Prov. 3:5–6).

With the Spirit as my guide, the words of God became a living and transforming instrument upon me. I was amazed, encouraged and, at times, thrown to my knees in tears and prayer and groaning as He revealed my past and the ways I had grieved Him. These moments were hard, but His grace sustained me. His love strengthened me. I was being disciplined by Him, at the pace I needed and to the degree I needed as I received His peace (Heb. 12:12).

In the days ahead, His Spirit led me in new directions—each day, each week, a step here, a step there. I remember going to see Alan Eason, our preacher at the time. Without judgment, he listened and prayed with me. Upon his advice, I attended Adult Children for Alcoholics (ACA), where I learned about the tendencies, the common sins, of children growing up with a parent addicted to alcohol. I remember that when I heard those behaviors read at the first meeting, I couldn't speak. When it came my turn to introduce myself, l sat there in silence.

I attended the ACA sessions until I went to a church growth seminar in Atlanta with Alan and the elders of our church. There we learned to develop small groups to support one another in life, which we did. Sheila and I helped to lead the effort and, along with others, started a group in our home.

We began our first meeting with the Bible and a study called "Equipping the Saints," which we had brought back from Atlanta. In the first week, we wrote down the changes we needed to make with God as we could best express them. We shared these with each other. What I most remember about the next four years were the prayers. At the end of being together each week, we prayed for one another. These prayers were honest and from our spirits and in the Spirit.

At another important time of confession and pain, Susie, a sister in Christ, told Sheila and I about her journey of discovery and growth through fasting. She told us to read Isaiah 58, which we did and to commit ourselves to a season of transformation by fasting once a day for six months. I now remember those days of discomfort as special gifts from God and they continued His road of discipline for me. They gradually reset my mind on things above as I learned to live life in the new way of the Spirit.

In those days and years, He taught me that His temple is within me. I carried Him with me and He filled me with His Spirit in moments of testimony and work for His kingdom. When I dedicated everything to Him, this was His revival for me. A business, Interactive Communications, became IC (in Christ) with a logo of a stick figure in a crimson image. Invoices began with 3 (denoting Father, Son and Spirit). Every communication tip and life lesson I taught came from the Bible. My business became a ministry for spreading the life and lessons of Jesus.

I found other brothers and sisters within many denominations across America. Five of us began ministering to young men through manhood weekends, "Men's Gatherings." This continued for 15 years as men traveled across America. Many found Jesus. Others began their own personal revivals and families were changed forever. (We're all ministers of a new covenant of grace. Find your place in the fields in His work and your joy will increase.)

Somehow, in our miracle, the Father allowed us to keep our home. I'm not the same person. He's changed me and continues to make me new every day through the Spirit of God, my advocate, my comforter, my strength—Jesus.

This Week

- Pray in the Spirit . . .

  "But Jesus often withdrew to lonely places and prayed" (Luke 5:16).

- Repent of sin . . .

  "Godly sorrow brings repentance that leads to salvation and leaves no regret, but worldly sorrow brings death" (2 Cor. 7:10). "The Lord is not slow in keeping his promise, as some understand slowness. He is patient with you, not wanting anyone to perish, but everyone to come to repentance" (2 Pet. 3:9).

- Meditate on His word . . .

  "But his delight is in the law of the Lord, and on his law he meditates day and night" (Psa. 1:2). "Within your temple, O God, we meditate on your unfailing love" (Psa. 48:9). "I will meditate on all your works and consider all your mighty deeds" (Psa. 77:12). My eyes stay open through the watches of the night, that I may meditate on your promises" (Psa. 119:148).

- Reset your mind . . .

  "Set your minds on things above, not on earthly things" (Col. 3:2). "Those who live according to the sinful nature have their minds set on what that nature desires; but those who live in accordance with the Spirit have their minds set on what the Spirit desires" (Rom. 8:5).

· Fast in His presence . . .

"'How is it that we and the Pharisees fast, but your disciples do not fast?' Jesus answered, "How can the guests of the bridegroom mourn while he is with them? The time will come when the bride-groom will be taken from them; then they will fast" (Matt. 9:14–15)

· Minister in the fields (with all of us) . . .

"He told them, "The harvest is plentiful, but the workers are few. Ask the Lord of the harvest, therefore, to send out workers into his harvest field" (Luke 10:2).

"He has made us competent as ministers of a new covenant—not of the letter but of the Spirit; for the letter kills, but the Spirit gives life" (2 Cor. 3:6).

"And you will be called priests of the Lord, you will be named ministers of our God" (Is. 61:6).

• • • •

Part III

A NEW CREATION
IN THE SPIRIT OF GOD

discussions and groaning . . .

A spiritual sage of long ago sat by himself and mused, in secret, how long conversations should be between people. As a learned man, his time was important and he wanted to just say what needed to be said and go on to other more important matters. When someone approached him that day, he pondered to himself, I should greet them, but how? So, he thought, I'll just say, "Hello," then no, shorter still, I'll say, "Hi." But then he decided, Let them say something first, and I'll respond if necessary. Even so, he quickly realized they might go on without a word. What to do? He thought the same about speaking with God—short, long, morning, evening, a few words or many, or just stay silent until He spoke to him? . . .

. . . Then the Spirit interceded and, as he knelt to pray, groaned for him. He comforted him and reminded him in this way, "He loves you when you talk with Him in Spirit and in truth, in humility, in forgiveness of others, without losing heart, with few words or many, in tears or in awe, on all kinds of occasions out of love for His Son. Seek Him in secret, pray in your spirit, and don't be surprised if you don't know what to say and how to say it." The Spirit will come alongside and make your desires known to your

Father. Just bring yourself to Him—He'll do the rest and will give you rest.

On all kinds of occasions and throughout the day, look for Him—talk with Him—walk with Him. Do this both by yourself and with others.

14

DEEPER STILL: THE HOLY SPIRIT GROANING WITH OUR SPIRITS

In the same way, the Spirit helps us in our weakness. *We do not know what we ought to pray for, but the Spirit himself intercedes for us with groans that words cannot express.* And he who searches our hearts knows the mind of the Spirit, because the Spirit intercedes for the saints in accordance with God's will. (Rom. 8:26–27)

There was something about the prayers of Jesus that caused the disciples to ask Him to teach them to pray—something different from the scribes and Pharisees. We don't know what they saw in Jesus when He prayed, but the prayer we they did hear him pray was simple, short and contained requests like: "Your kingdom come," a submissive petition for His "daily bread" and for "forgiveness." (Matt. 6:9-15) Matthew, Mark, Luke and John record many times that they would see Him withdraw in solitude, often into the mountains, to pray to God. They heard Him tell all of them:

> And when you pray, do not be like the hypocrites, for they love to pray standing in the synagogues and on the street corners to be seen by men. I tell you the truth, they have received their reward in full. But *when you pray, go into your room, close the door and pray to your Father, who is unseen.* Then *your Father, who sees what is done in secret, will reward you.* And when you pray, do not keep on babbling like pagans, for they think they will be heard because of their many words. (Matt. 6:5–7)

When Paul writes to the Corinthians in his first letter, he explains how they have been enriched in every way, with speaking, knowledge and all spiritual gifts. He begins his writing with a different approach than he does with the Ephesians or Galatians. He writes to young Christians living in the capital of the province, the largest and richest port—a city by the sea. Their worldliness concerns him and Paul knows there are divisions among them and a lack of love for one another. They are jealous of each other and quarrel over insignificant issues. Although blessed with gifts of the Spirit and living with surplus, they lack humility and unity.

Paul tells them to stop boasting and to remember God's temple within them—to crucify their pride and to use their gifts from the Spirit for the common good. He wants them to live as new creations reborn by the Spirit of God—given to them because of their belief in Christ Jesus, who was crucified for their sins. He wants them to live a life of sacrificial love in the Spirit and in service to each other as a testimony to those who need Him.

After describing love to them (1 Cor. 13), Paul continues a letter to them by explaining the proper uses of their gifts. He begins in this way: "Follow the way of love and eagerly desire spiritual gifts, especially the gift of prophecy." (1 Cor. 15:1)

Regarding praying in the Spirit, he says:

> Follow the way of love and eagerly desire spiritual gifts, especially the gift of prophecy. For anyone who speaks in a tongue does not speak to men but to God. Indeed, *no one understands him; he utters mysteries with his spirit*. But everyone who prophesies speaks to men for their strengthening, encouragement and comfort. (1 Cor. 14:1–3)

> For if I pray in a tongue, *my spirit prays*, but *my mind is unfruitful*. So what shall I do? *I will pray with my spirit*, but *I will also pray with my mind; I will sing with my spirit*, but *I will also sing with my mind*. (1 Cor. 14:14–15)

> If there is no interpreter, *the speaker should keep quiet in the church and speak to himself and God*. (1 Cor. 14:28)

I believed what the Bible says about spiritual gifts, but didn't have a personal experience with praying or singing in the Spirit, where I utter "mysteries with my spirit." So, I turned to two people I trust, my sister-in-law, Denisa, and my dear friend Joe Blackburn. I asked them to explain to me how the gift of praying in the Spirit occurred in their lives, what it is, when they do it and what it means to them. Joe and Denisa describe what Paul describes as a private utterance and as their "prayer language" given to them by the Spirit of God.

Denisa Cooper: Her Prayer Language

"I always said that I was born to pray! I was praying to a God long before I even knew Him! So you can imagine when I finally came to know my Heavenly Father at the age of 36, what a glorious reunion it was. And, I have to say that I have never felt the 'lull' that some people say happened to them. I have been 'on fire' for Him realizing that prayer is a privilege, not an obligation, and through it I could have an incredible relationship with the Creator of heaven and Earth.

"Now with that said, I will tell you I am not the most 'biblical scholar' you will meet. I can't turn to verses like some people can nor am I the best at memorizing. But I can tell you stories over and over again of answered prayer. I can tell you how our Father hears every prayer—not only hears but answers every prayer you ask. I can speak of miracles that I have witnessed and that I have been a part of because of prayer. I am a warrior of prayer.

"One Sunday, our pastor taught on praying in the Spirit, or in our prayer language. I was not tuned in to this form of prayer until I started worshiping with the Church of the Savior in Nicholasville, Kentucky. The first time I heard people praying in the Spirit, it actually startled me to the point I went and spoke to the pastor about it. Not understanding what was going on was a hindrance because without understanding it, how could I possibly want to participate. Anyway, after the teaching, he invited anyone that was interested in receiving this 'gift' and would like to be prayed over to come on down. I went.

"We went into a private room where several leaders divided us into groups and spoke to us. My group leader explained that praying in the Spirit allows the Holy Spirit to pray over areas and things that we don't know about or don't know how to pray about. Many many times in my life I have not known 'how to pray.' I now understand this form of prayer as a way to keep my thoughts in line with God's thoughts. She then prayed over us and encouraged us to start praying and let the words just come out . . . Well it didn't happen for me. Not then, anyway!

"While I was disappointed, I remember she had mentioned praying in the Spirit while singing. So, one day, soon thereafter, I was walking and started singing and the words just poured out! Now at that time, I'm not sure I would call them words, as they sounded like a 'garbled sound that was confusing and distorted.' They still sound like that but now I understand that they are not necessarily for me to understand. They are God, in the Spirit, praying for things that need prayer for—for requests that I might not be privy to. They are prayers that reach the depth of God's heart. And that is one place I desire to be—to be aligned with my Father!

"There are some special times that I like to 'pray in the Spirit.' One is when I am with a group of brothers/sisters in Christ and some are praying in their prayer language. At other times, it is during worship (singing) and sometimes it is while someone is praying. Recently, during prayer with others, silence came over us and, instead of ending our prayer time, we whispered in our language . . . that was really special, as we so felt His presence. And then there are the times that I feel a prompting that I should pray in the Spirit. Those are the times that, by obeying God, you will learn more about Him than you will ever learn in a study!

"There's no right or wrong way to pray in the Spirit. Ask the Lord for His gift of a prayer language. And know that having a prayer language doesn't make you more spiritual or more religious! It is just another way of praying. Believe that your praying in the Spirit is perfect and desirable and exactly what our Heavenly Father wants more than anything—a conversation with you!"

Joe Blackburn: His Prayer Language

"Around 1980, my first wife left the Baptist Church and we were attending a new church. It was called Trinity Chapel, which was a non-denominational church in inner-city Knoxville. This was during the time of the charismatic renewal sweeping the nation. For a man who had run from God for 22 years (I first accepted Christ when I was 9 years old) and was reared in a Southern Baptist church, what I experienced was hardly normal. I remember folks in Trinity Chapel having such joy in church. They were so in love with Christ that it seemed like He was their best friend. They didn't even use hymnals to sing. Prior to going to Trinity, most Christians I had met in the past were without joy and so somber 'they could eat corn from a coke bottle.'

"At Trinity, there were folks who occasionally would speak in an unknown tongue. I was told it was called the 'Baptism of the Holy Spirit.' It was beyond weird and I wanted nothing to do with them or this so called 'gift.' I told my wife that under no circumstance did I want to be hugged by men in the church with them babbling words I couldn't understand.

"Nevertheless, I occasionally attended the church and even coached the women's softball team. I was intrigued by but far from sold on this 'new' type of church.

"My wife soon volunteered to sing in the choir. And once she invited her parents, who were very devoted Southern Baptists, to attend the Easter music program. My job was to be their host and sit with them. I prayed, 'God please don't let any of these wackos do something weird.' Wouldn't you know it that after the concert there was a public message in tongues, which was followed by an interpretation in English (totally scriptural by the way). I just about croaked. I thought—thanks a lot, God. I coped by acting like it never happened. It is amazing the things God does to get your attention and torpedo your pride.

"In January 1982, my wife was diagnosed with breast cancer at the age of 34. During her stay in the hospital, I spent considerable time in the hospital chapel reading the Bible and feebly attempting to pray for her. I realized that I had reached a place within my arrogant pride that I thought would never occur. I couldn't go through it, over it or around it. In short, I couldn't fix this life-threatening problem we found ourselves in. I had to depend on God for the first time since I was a youth.

"While she was in surgery, I went back to the chapel to pray again. When I entered the room, the power of the Holy Spirit was so strong that I fell on my face asking for forgiveness and another chance to serve Him.

"God's response was one of grace and total forgiveness. Waves of liquid love flowed over me again and again. I promised God that, with His help, I would never walk away again.

"The change in me was immediate and profound. My father later told me that when I came into the surgery waiting room, he hardly recognized me. My countenance had changed, my language had changed, my thought life and my desires—everything about me had changed. I was a new creature in Christ.

"A couple of days after my wife's surgery some visitors from the church came to visit. I shared the story of the chapel encounter with the Lord. One of the men asked if I would like to receive the baptism of the Holy Spirit. My response was that I would take any gift God was willing to give. He laid his hands on me and prayed that I would receive my 'prayer language. (Note: there are different beliefs held about receiving a 'prayer language.' Some people say it happens when you first receive the baptism, while other folks say it can happen later. Mine happened several months later. It started slowly then occurred more and more—like a dam crumbling under water pressure. I have heard it said that our first baptism [repentance] is for us. The second baptism is for the power to help others. (Acts 19:1–6)

"That was over 39 years ago. More than ever it is a precious and, I believe, vital gift in my walk with Christ. I admittedly don't know how and what to pray for at many times. I believe the use of my prayer language helps me pray for my wife, family, other people and ministry needs. It has become a special part of my daily devotions (quiet time). It is a gift for all who desire it (1 Corinthians 12:10 and Acts 4:31). I believe as we rapidly race towards the end of time, there's even more need for wisdom and discernment to boldly battle against the evil one and his plans. Praying in the Spirit is an important tool in the arsenal of the believer. We need God's power like never before."

> Is any one of you in trouble? *He should pray.* Is anyone happy? Let him sing songs of praise. Is any one of you sick? He should *call the elders of the church to pray over him and anoint him with oil in the name of the Lord. And the prayer offered in faith will make the sick person well; the Lord will raise him up.* If he has sinned, he will be forgiven. Therefore *confess your sins to each other and pray for each other so that you may be healed. The prayer of a righteous man is powerful and effective.* (Jas 5:13–16)

This Week

- "Pray in the Spirit on all occasions with all kinds of prayers and requests. With this in mind, be alert and always keep on praying for all the saints" (Eph. 6:18). Do this by name if possible for those you know, and then do this for the Christ believers throughout the world.

- Especially do this for those with whom you have had disagreements or for those you need to forgive. Tell God about how you were hurt, how it felt and ask Him to heal you of the pain and any remaining malice toward those who harmed you. In submission to the Spirit, release your bitterness and pray for blessings in their lives through His power within you.

- As for praying, singing and speaking in tongues or other gifts of the Spirit, please study with me 1 Corinthians 12 and 14; Romans 12:4–8; and Ephesians 4:1-11. We'll discuss what we learn as the Lord guides us into all truth. In the meantime, if you're moved by Him, ask for the Spirit to give you a prayer language to be used in your private time with God. (You may want to listen to this Max Lucado interview here: (https://www.youtube.com/live/zKdBn2e_Omw?si=0YXPbXmgoX7LYPh6) In it, Max explains how, in 2018, he received this private time gift of a heavenly language. As he answers questions with humility, you can discover what this gift means to him.)

For if I pray in a tongue, my spirit prays, but my mind is unfruitful. So what shall I do? *I will pray with my spirit,* but I will also pray with my mind; *I will sing with my spirit*, but I will also sing with my mind. (1 Cor. 14:14–15)

If there is no interpreter, the speaker should keep quiet in the church and *speak to himself and God."* (1 Cor. 14:28)

• • • •

for the common good . . .

*A poet once thought, I'll write about Jack and Jill
going up the hill today, and as he began, he thought
about leaving out Jack. Yet, in all the lines he'd write
on this very special day, the words when read out
clanged in a discordant way. Jill, pill, will—it was
humor nil. So, he brought back Jack, who fell down
the hill and Jill came tumbling after . . . and all was
well, the water in the pail, and the ensuing laughter.*

*But what if Frodo didn't need Sam, or the pitcher
didn't need a catcher, or if Mary had a pig and didn't
want the lamb? What if a man only heard himself
and cared not for his bride? What if there was a
bow without an arrow, or a hammer and no nail?
Or an orchestra playing without a conductor or an
audience? What if the poet didn't know he could
rhyme words in his poem and Jack and Jill went up a
mountain and not a hill to fetch a pail of sand?*

*And, so it goes with any Christian body in which
people do not seek to know their spiritual gifts or, if
they do, then use them in a discordant way.*

Do not be ignorant of spiritual gifts. There are many but one Spirit. While all of them are valued, eagerly seek the greater gifts. Eagerly seek the gift of prophecy. Eagerly seek to strengthen, encourage and comfort others. Eagerly seek love. (see 1 Cor. 12-14)

THE GIFTS OF THE SPIRIT FOR THE COMMON GOOD 1

When my son played baseball, I was able to watch a very talented sports team travel from city to city for its games. It was coached by a former pitcher of a prestigious college baseball school with a well-known tradition for winning.

I believe the coach meant well, but his outwardly displayed arrogance and need to win caused him to berate his young son. He also treated some of the less gifted kids in a demanding and humiliating way. This caused rifts among the parents and his assistant coach. Without realizing it, he depended upon his own knowledge and giftedness. His manners and demeanor with the kids screamed out, "I don't like you when you fail; you're less than I need you to be. See me, I'm more important than you!" Wrestling with his own need for identity, the desire to win gave way to losses—losses for his family and failing to express loving concern for the kids he coached.

Years before, the apostle Paul began his letter to the Corinthian church thankful to God for the grace given them in Christ Jesus. But he sees something different and concerning about this family of believers. In their walk with the Spirit, Jesus gives them an abundance of spiritual gifts, which implies that this abundance might not have been present in every church: they did not "lack any spiritual gift" (1 Cor. 1:7).

But there's a problem. Divisions exist among them and they quarrel about which leader each of them follows. Even with all their spiritual gifts, knowledge and many talented speakers, they argue with one another. Paul sees a lack of love and unity.

Paul writes that not many of them are "wise by human standards, influential or of noble birth" (1 Cor 1:26). He further explains he didn't come to them with eloquence or superior wisdom or courage or strength. He didn't speak with wise and persuasive words as he testified about Jesus and Him crucified, but with a demonstration of the Spirit's power (1 Cor 2:1–4).

Knowing that He'll be writing to them about their sins, their immaturity and the proper and improper use of their gifts, Paul tells them that they didn't receive the spirit of the world, but the Spirit who is from God. He explains that those without the Spirit don't accept the things that come from the Spirit, "for they are foolishness to him, and he cannot understand them, because they are spiritually discerned" (1 Cor. 2:14).

Paul describes the Corinthians as worldly, arrogant, grumbling, sexually immoral and dishonoring their bodies. They have forgotten that their bodies are temples of the Holy Spirit and that they were bought with the price of Christ's blood. They have forgotten that the world is passing away in its present form. Paul tells them to "be careful" not to fall and to "flee from idolatry" (1 Cor. 10:12-14).

Stepping Back and Looking at the Bigger Picture

In his letter to the Ephesians, Paul shows his concern for "the faithful in Christ Jesus" (Eph. 1:1). He knows that the people of this body of believers work hard, persevere and don't tolerate wicked men. He knows they have endured hardships and haven't grown weary, but have fallen from a great height and need to repent of forsaking their first love—Jesus and His salvation. He reminds them that they had been separated from God and that it is by grace they have been saved through Christ.

Paul prays on his knees that they be strengthened with power through the Father's Spirit in their inner being (Eph. 3:16). At the end of his letter, he writes to tell them their battle is not against flesh and blood but against the powers and principalities in the heavenly realms. He wants them to be strong in the Lord and in His mighty power, knowing the truth; righteous in Him alone, faithful and saved by Jesus; holding onto the word of God and praying in the Spirit on all occasions. Then, they will not lose their first love and fall into legalistic efforts like the Galatians.

The people in Corinth believe in Christ but the powers and principalities have gained a foothold. Pride and sin have entered the Corinthian fellowship. They have faith. They have manifestations of the Spirit's power, but Paul wants to remind them that while faith and hope are important, all the gifts of the Spirit must be administered for the common good and in love and unity among the saints. To make his point clear, he first describes the gifts and their uses among the body for the common good:

> Now about spiritual gifts, brothers, *I do not want you to be ignorant* . . .
>
> There are different kinds of gifts, but the same Spirit. There are different kinds of service, but the same Lord. There are different kinds of working, but the same God works all of them in all men.
>
> *Now to each one the manifestation of the Spirit is given for the common good.*
>
> To one there is given through the Spirit *the message of wisdom*, to another *the message of knowledge* by means of the same Spirit, to another *faith* by the same Spirit, to another *gifts of healing* by that one Spirit, to another *miraculous powers*, to another *prophecy*, to another *distinguishing between spirits*, to another *speaking in different kinds of tongues*, and to still another *the interpretation of tongues*.
>
> *All these are the work of one and the same Spirit*, and *he gives them to each one, just as he determines*. (1 Cor. 12:1, 4–11)

- "I do not want you to be ignorant."
- "To each one the manifestation of the Spirit is given for the common good."
- "He gives to each one, just as he determines."

As he writes, Paul continues to explain that a body of believers is a unit of many parts, baptized by one Spirit. Each has equal importance. Each unified with the others—each suffering as the others—each rejoicing with the honors of the others. One body, one Spirit, one love. Before he talks about love in great detail, he finishes His description of spiritual titles and gifts that exist within the body:

> Now you are the body of Christ, and each one of you is a part of it. And in the church God has appointed first of all apostles, second prophets, third teachers, then workers of miracles, also those having gifts of healing, those able to help others, those with gifts of administration, and those speaking in different kinds of tongues.
>
> Are all apostles? Are all prophets? Are all teachers? Do all work miracles? Do all have gifts of healing? Do all speak in tongues? Do all interpret? But eagerly desire the greater gifts. And now I will show you the most excellent way. (1 Cor. 12:27–31)

> We have different gifts, according to the grace given us. If a man's gift is prophesying, let him use it in proportion to his faith.
>
> If it is serving, let him serve; if it is teaching, let him teach; if it is encouraging, let him encourage;
>
> if it is contributing to the needs of others, let him give generously; if it is leadership, let him govern diligently; if it is showing mercy, let him do it cheerfully. (Rom. 12:6–8)

> It was he who gave some to be *apostles*, some to be *prophets*, some to be *evangelists*, and some to be *pastors*

and *teachers*, to prepare God's people for works of service, so that the body of Christ may be built up until we all reach unity in the faith and in the knowledge of the Son of God and become mature, attaining to the whole measure of the fullness of Christ. (Eph. 4:11–13)

A Thought About Our Current State

The people of the world have been wounded by sin, by physical ailments, by disease. Their minds have harmful thoughts, grievances and bitterness. Modern medicine and psychology seek to help—to touch and treat a person in such a way that they are helped. Like other scientific approaches to life, they are important but have their limits—especially when they try to protect against or remedy evil, sin, demonic oppression and powers and principalities.

(Note: I respect doctors and psychiatrists who understand the physical and mental sciences. I also wish, when needed and when given a choice, that I might find a spiritual doctor or spiritual psychologist to treat me—someone with great faith in God, someone who depends upon prayer and who believes in the Spirit and the miracles of God—someone who believes and knows the word of God.)

I need people praying for me. I need people speaking into my life and helping me discern between good and evil. I need people of faith and wisdom. I need people who pray for the healing and the repairing of my soul. I need people who listen to God and are willing to help me understand myself and the direction best for me. I need the Spirit of God working through the body of believers to remind me of His words and truth, and I will seek these things from believers in Christ.

The gifts of the Spirit are manifested for the common good. They are as follows (1 Cor. 12:7):

- *Wisdom:* **σοφος** (*sophos*)—wise; i.e., useful practical skills (financial, food, exercise, relationships, etc.) and knowledge of God's observable reality (how to get from points A to B in a way that the Spirit wants for our life).
- *Knowledge:* **γνωσις** (*gnōsis*)—to know (even *intimately*); to have and handle information in one's mind for the benefit of helping others; used in the sense of knowing a person and their spiritual and emotional needs.
- *Faith:* **πιστις** (*pistis*)—faith or sureness; trust or certainty in God, the love and salvation of Jesus and the guidance of the Spirit to a better life.
- *Healings:* **ιαματων** (*iamatōn*)—of healings, curings; repairing (the soul), remedy.
- *Miracles:* **ενεργηματα δυναμεων** (*energēmata dynameōn*) an effect or (inner) working or operation of the Spirit in a miraculous (mighty/powerful) way.
- *Prophecy:* **προφητεια** (*prophēteia*)—as a speaker, a teacher or a person divinely making clear the word or the will of God, for today or tomorrow, about a culture or a person or a group of people; an assertion or prediction; a glimpse into the future (revealed truth about something): "Do this and this will happen."
- *Discernment (of spirits):* **διακρισεις πνευματων** (*diakriseis pneumatōn*)—a thorough judgment upon

something that "appears" the same; spiritually trained faculties knowing this "something" or person is of a good or bad spirit.

- *Tongues*: **γενη γλωσσων** (*genē glōssōn*)—different kinds of tongues with the same nature (earthly languages, private prayer language with God, etc.).
- *Interpretation (of tongues)*: **'ερμηνεια** (*hermēneia*)—to interpret, explain or translate, an intercessory ability to tell what is meant by the tongue/language that occurs from the divine—what is said between God's Spirit and a man's spirit.
- *Help*: **αντιληψις** (*antilēpsis*)—meaning a redirecting; a grabbing hold of someone working at something in order to provide a serving alternative, aid and strength to their, perhaps dismal, situation.
- *Administrations*: **κυβερνησεις** (*kybernēseis*)—steering, acting as a helmsman of a ship (church); to construct policies that help a body run smoothly.
- *Encouragement*: **παρακλησις** (*paraklēsis*)—a calling to one's aid; i.e., bringing spiritual encouragement from God's Spirit—maybe a holy urging and comforting.
- *Giving*: **μεταδιδωμι** (*metadidōmi*)—handing over items or sharing something you have; to bestow, share.
- *Showing mercy*: **'ελεεω** (*eleō*)—to have pity or mercy on; where expectations have not been met (because of spiritual, physical or mental impairment) as the Spirit leads the giver.
- *Leading*: **προϊστημι** (*proistēmi*)—ruling and protecting with great care.

The following are gifted positions by the Spirit for the purpose of preparing God's people for works of service, so that the body may be built up and reach a unity in their faith and knowledge of Jesus, each part doing its work and becoming mature and more like the King of kings. (Eph. 3:16)

- *Apostles*: **αποστολους** (*apostolous*)—those sent on a mission by God; thus commissioned to go with orders; called to go somewhere to advance the kingdom of God; placing something, perhaps a ministry in an intended position.
- *Prophets*: **προφητας** (*prophētas*)—persons gifted with bringing a divine truth into the lives of believers, giving an inspiration of God; sometimes for a particular situation; persons who may have a foretelling of the future; who pass on information from God to someone and about them.
- *Evangelists*: **ευαγγελιστας** (*euaggelistas*)—bringers of good news (the gospel); given this ability by the Spirit. While all Christians participate in this, the evangelist is led to see this as his vocation and does this by relating the message (the good news) to a person's needs and within their cultural understanding.
- *Shepherds*: **ποιμενας** (*poimenas*)—herdsmen, watching for enemies, defending Cjristians from spiritual attack; loving them; earning their trust by genuine concern; keeping them in the body of Christ.
- *Teachers*: **διδασκαλους** (*didaskalous*)—Spirit-enabled and gifted instructors who love to master

what they teach and have a genuine love for their hearers' growth.

Paul wants us to work together, each with a spiritual gift of service, so that we're "no longer like infants, tossed back and forth by the waves, and blown here and there by every wind of teaching and by the cunning and craftiness of men in their deceitful scheming." (Eph. 4:14). In the Spirit, we can do this!

Like the Corinthians, he expects us to live no longer as Gentiles do, in the futility of our thinking. He wants us to continue our growth, in prayer, and in the Spirit. He wants us to heighten our sensitivity to sin and sensuality and every kind of impurity, and *to be made new in the renewal of our minds.* The gifts he gives us all will cause us to live as children of the light. *In this way, we'll not grieve the Spirit of God.* (paraphrased and quoted from Eph. 4:7–30; Eph. 5:1)

This Week

- Please pray that the Spirit will lead you in your service to a body of believers. If you desire a particular gift, pray for it. Begin to increase your awareness of the Spirit's work in you and through you. You're the light of the world. His joy radiates from within you and upon those you see wherever you go.

- Ask yourself, "Do I pursue God in prayer and in my spirit (with sincerity and faith)?" This is the best place to begin a walk in the Spirit. Begin to offer "all occasions" (Eph. 6::18) to Him for His direction.

- This is a promise of God: if you lean on Him for your strength and guidance and transformation, He'll come to you in power and you will know His presence in your life. He'll direct your paths (Prov. 3:5–6).

- As we begin to complete this study, please *look for His power in and on your life*. When this becomes apparent, prepare (in prayer) to tell your children and those important to you. Then, ask Him to equip you to tell your brothers and sisters in the church and those you meet wherever you go. You will be a messenger of the good news!

  The eye cannot say to the hand, "I don't need you!" And the head cannot say to the feet, "I don't need you!" On the contrary, those parts of the body that seem to be weaker are indispensable, and the parts that we think are less honorable we treat with special honor. And the parts that are unpresentable are treated with special modesty, while our presentable parts need no special treatment. But God has combined the members of the body and has given greater honor to the parts that lacked it, so that *there should be no division in the body*, but that *its parts should have equal concern for each other. If one part suffers, every part suffers with it; if one part is honored, every part rejoices with it.* (1 Cor. 12:21–26)

. . . .

strangely true . . .

It's September, and a young college teacher takes his 8-year-old boy, Ryan, to the first day of class at a local university. As the adults there introduce themselves while sitting in their seats, one after the other all eventually turn to look at Ryan, who is next. His father asks him, "And, who are you?" His son replies, "Ryan." "What are you, Ryan?" his father continues. To which Ryan responds with one word: "Special!" His father then asks, "Are you weird?" "Yes," Ryan, without hesitation, answers.

Are you also weird? Are you a one-of-a-kind, wonderfully made child of God? Are you special?

Yes! Whether you feel this or not, it's true. You are special. There's no one like you and God loves what He's made. Our sins, abuse and rejection from others, and being treated like a number or a valueless thing does not change this fact. If you need the final proof, look at Jesus on the cross and see your name written on His bloodstained and broken body, alone, separated from His father, and dying for you—who will one day become His friend.

May the grace of the Lord Jesus Christ, and the love of God, and the fellowship of the Holy Spirit be with you all. (2 Cor. 13:14)

16

THE GIFTS OF THE SPIRIT FOR THE COMMON GOOD 2

Paul finishes his great discourse about love in his letter to the Corinthians with the words "And now these three remain: faith, hope and love. But the greatest of these is love" (1 Cor. 13:13).

I think that each day I live, God reveals another facet, like the cuts in a diamond, of what love really means. Obviously, despite their gifts, the Corinthians needed some serious growth in this area. They were like the rich whom Jesus mentioned—who needed to think more soberly of their lower position in the kingdom while realizing the high position of the poor. It's difficult to do things for the common good when you have a lot to understand about love and its intimate and profound impact on the life of the rich and poor.

Jennifer Judy "JJ" Heller writes and sings American and Christian folk music. In 2010, she wrote "What Love Really Means." Sheila and I think she captured the heart of those who look for someone to love them for who they are and not for what they have done or what they will become. What Love Really Means . . . by JJ Heller . . . https://youtu.be/PgGUKWiw7Wk

What if you are a child whom no one wants, who has a story no one believes? What if you pray to God every night for Him to send someone to love you?

Or, what if you are a woman who works in an office who feels as if it's "shrinking" from one day to the next? As each day ends, you go to the gym, but a mirror reveals your body wasting away. You dream about a man who left you and wonder if you'd been thinner or prettier: "Maybe he'd have stayed."

What if you are a prisoner in a jail somewhere remote, where the sounds echo with sadness. You see your past filled with lies and murder and deep within your soul regret what you've done. Your cry of forgiveness echoes within the walls of the prison and you want to go home. You want the Lord to come and get you.

JJ reminds us of ourselves and of the desperate souls around us who hurt for love deep inside and whom no one sees or cares about. She tells us that most everyone wants someone to love them and to show them "what love really means."

Over and over again, the song's chorus helps us remember that God will love and will give us the love we never knew. He'll love us for us, not for our future, not for our looks, not for our accomplishments, but for us, as His children—each special in our own ways.

Do you know this kind of love? Does someone love you for you? Does anyone really see you? God does and He wants you to love him. He'll bless you when you mourn and He'll comfort you. When you are poor in your spirit, He'll live within you. When your heart is troubled, He'll be with you. He'll be all you'll need. He'll be within you to comfort, encourage, strengthen and help you understand His love for you.

Years ago, when my father had his first heart attack, my mom left me with my brothers. We were scared and alone. She went to the hospital to meet my dad, who had just arrived on a plane from New York where he had been working. We went to their room at home and got onto their bed and prayed to God. He met us there.

Years ago, at 2:00 a.m., I knelt and prayed for God to let me keep my family, and if he wanted our house and everything else to take them. I wanted Him only to let me keep my family. My laziness in life, my lack of responsibility and my sins had led all of us to this moment. I prayed for His forgiveness and His peace and His mercy. He gave them and walked with me through the discipline I needed to be a better man.

Everyone needs to know that Jesus loves them—really loves them. They will look for Him in your attitudes and behaviors. So, follow the way of love and eagerly desire spiritual gifts, and especially the gift of prophecy; for you will speak to all around you for their "strengthening, encouragement and comfort." Do this and you will edify the church of Christ. (1 Cor. 14:1, 3-4)

prophecy: προφητης (prophētēs)—as a speaker, a teacher or a person, through the Spirit, making clear the word or the will of God, for today or tomorrow, about a culture or a person or a group of people; an assertion or prediction—glimpse into the future (revealed truth about something); i.e., do this and this will happen.

The Restoration of John Ritchie's Soul (by John Ritchie)

"In late summer of 1989, I found myself going through a divorce, without employment and moving to my parents' home. I cold-turkey stopped using alcohol as my chosen anesthetic and had to face all the pain without it. A doctor friend and a psychologist both told me I would be dead within a year because the pain would be too great to bear. Since I was without hope, that was "the good news."

"I had gone to church in my earlier life, but since then my lifestyle had spat in God's face for 20-plus years. Seeking Him didn't seem to be an option.

"I visited a psychologist and, after sharing my situation with her, she said she had never seen anyone in my condition. She told me she could see all the way through me as if I had no soul left. I lied and told her I was OK even though I was planning to commit suicide that night. After surviving the night, events began to occur that were nothing short of miraculous.

"I had dinner with Lance Cooper, who had been brought into my company to train my salespeople. After detailing my situation, including what the psychologist had told me, he smiled and, I think, laughed at me from across the table, and for no apparent reason said, "You're going to be OK." This gave me a small shred of hope even though there was no evidence this was true.

"Later that week, I went to a scheduled health insurance exam. During the appointment, the young nurse, in her early twenties, asked how I was doing. I told her I had had better days. She asked if I was going to church, and I told her I was thinking about it. Then suddenly, out of nowhere, she asked if I had ever given my life to Jesus. This caught me so by surprise I lied and said I was thinking about that as well.

"She asked if I would like for her to pray with me and to do it right now. I was so startled I said, 'Yes.' In my condition what could it hurt?

"When she prayed a simple prayer, she was sweating so much that the sweat ran down our clasped hands and puddled on the floor. She told me she had never done anything like that in her life. Later, I tried to find her to thank her, but it was like she had disappeared. Someone once asked me if I thought she was an angel.

"Lance called me back and told me that he had been praying about me and wanted me to move to Knoxville. He said that he wanted me to come to church with him so I could get healed. He also hired me into his company.

"I moved to Knoxville on New Year's Day of 1990 into a long-stay hotel knowing no one but Lance. I went to his house that day armed with an old King James Bible I had found to attend a small-group Bible study. I attended many of these in many homes as people studied and prayed—prayed for each other and prayed for me.

"That was the beginning of a totally transformed me. There have been so many movements of the Spirit in my life since, it would be difficult to document all of them. Many have been far outside my human logic but have taught me to look for the Holy Spirit in all circumstances and even if I don't understand, to be confident in Him and His leading.

But the Counselor, the Holy Spirit, whom the Father will send in my name,will teach you all things and will remind you of everything I have said to you. Peace I leave with you; my peace I give you. I do not give to you as the world gives. Do not let your hearts be troubled and do not be afraid. (John 14:26–27)

The Prophetic Revelation of Samuel (by Alan Eason)

"Often, since I became a Christian at age 17, I have had the sense that God was showing me things. This happened sometimes when praying but more often it happened in vivid dreams.

"One of those dreams was of having a son. In the dream I saw him at age 1, age 5 and age 21. I still have the clear picture in my mind. He had dark hair and green eyes, like my wife to be, Natalia, has. I awoke with such a clear vision that I felt it must surely be a vision, not just a wishful dream.

"That was before Natalia and I were even married, but were already engaged. She was still in Brazil. More on that at another time.

"But this story is about something beyond dreams or visions, as subjective as they can be (and I am always something of a skeptic). This story is about two overt 'prophecies,' unbidden and totally unexpected, from two separate people who approached Natalia separately within the space of 20 minutes. It happened over two years after my dream.

"Natalia and I were married in the States. Because of difficulties with the immigration and visa processes, we decided to marry here rather than in her home country of Brazil. It was also not possible to get her family to the States for the wedding, so we had a wedding in Oak Ridge at a cousin's home with only my family and our friends present. That was in May, 2002.

"As wonderful as that wedding was, we also wanted to have a wedding (celebration at least) in Brazil with her large extended family. We got that chance around Christmastime in 2003. With my mother also accompanying us, we flew to Natalia's home city in Brazil, Vitoria da Conquista. Her family was preparing a large wedding for 70 or more people with lots of festivities (they were all joking and calling it our 'Greek Wedding,' after the popular movie from the time).

"They also asked the preacher from one of the local evangelical churches they attended to do our Brazilian-version 'wedding.' Once we had arrived and settled with Natalia's parents, we decided to attend the pastor's church on a Thursday evening and get to know him. The wedding was still a couple of days away.

"I need to stop now and give you a very significant backstory. Natalia and I had not been trying to have children the first year or so of our marriage. We knew we should not wait long, as I was already 50 and she was in her early thirties. But we were not worried about it then.

"On the night we were at the church, Pastor Edilson introduced us to the hundred or so people in the audience. He told them that he was going to do our wedding and welcomed us to the church. The audience was very gracious.

"At the end of the service, as we were standing up to leave, a woman who had been sitting behind Natalia tapped her on the shoulder. 'Can I talk to you for a minute?' she asked Nati, almost whispering, in Portuguese. 'I don't know you and am uncomfortable talking to you about this, but the Holy Spirit bothered me to say this to you: "You don't need to worry, because you're going to have your little baby."'

"Natalia does tend to worry, and this is how she describes that moment: 'I froze and wondered, *Why is she saying that? My first thought was, Oh No, we're going to have problems conceiving a child. We're not even thinking of having a child yet. We're newlyweds.*'

"Nati translated what she said to me right there, and told me that no one in the family even knew this lady. She was just sitting there in the church and tapped Nati's shoulder. I thought it pretty strange too.

"A few minutes later we went to the front of the church to meet the pastor, and another woman grabbed Natalia and hugged her. This lady was someone Nati's mother knew, and was known in the church as a prayer warrior who often prayed loudly for people, laid her hands on people, etcetera. Nati said that she had the reputation of being 'a little kooky, maybe' but she was a simple woman and very devout.

"As she hugged Nati, she said, 'You don't need to worry about your baby!' Nati just about freaked out and thought, *Why are they saying that to me?*

"We had no question in our minds at that time about having a child. We had not thought much about it. We were getting ready for our Brazilian wedding celebration.

"This strange occurrence sort of faded from our minds, but not totally.

"Fast forward to September of 2004. By now, we had made up our minds and had been trying to have a child for about five months, with no luck. But we were still not worried, it was not a long time since we had begun. Nevertheless, I decided to visit a urologist and be tested, given my age.

"The report was bad. There was not much likelihood on my side. The count was far too low. It was a very heavy blow.

"We visited the doctors again two weeks later and asked how we could improve our chances. We were ready to hear any possible suggestions they might have. The doctors told us during that sad conference that our best options would be adoption, or to try and get some 'in vitro' efforts going, though they were very expensive and not covered by our insurance. We walked out of that office in a state of shock and drove to the lake and parked there and wept and prayed and then prayed some more.

"It was now early October, 2004.

"We did remember what the two women had told Natalia in Brazil and, looking back, Nati remembers, "The only thing I had to hold onto was what those two women in my mother's church had told me almost a year before. What was God doing? Where was He?

"We spent a couple of very sad and depressed weeks, until Nati missed her period. She took a simple home test, and came running into my home office screaming, 'It says I'm pregnant!'

"We couldn't believe it though, until we went to an obstetrician in Knoxville and he let us listen on doppler to a beautiful heartbeat at 175 beats per minute. He smiled, 'You're going to have a baby.' Nati was seven to eight weeks along. The baby had already been conceived at the time we had sat in the urologists' office two weeks prior.

"In June of 2005, our son, Samuel (his name is from the Hebrew 'God Answers') was born. At age 1, he looked just like the boy I had seen in my dream before Nati and I even married. The only difference was, his eyes were brown by then. But they had been green when he was born."

Paul's twelve commands regarding the use of gifts for the common good:

1. "Follow the way of love and eagerly desire spiritual gifts . . . excel in gifts that build up the church" (1 Cor. 14:1, 12).
2. Especially desire the gift of prophecy. Be eager to prophesy. Prophesy to speak words that strengthen, encourage and comfort and to edify the church (1 Cor. 14:1, 3–4, 39).
3. "[A]nyone who speaks in a tongue should pray that he may interpret what he says" (1 Cor. 14:13).
4. "When you come together, everyone has a hymn, or word of instruction, a revelation, a tongue or an interpretation. All of these must be done for the strengthening of the church" (1 Cor. 14:26).
5. Only two or at most three, and one at a time, should speak in a tongue as someone interprets (1 Cor. 14:27).
6. "If there is no interpreter, the speaker should keep quiet in the church and speak to himself and God [privately]" (1 Cor. 14:28).
7. "Two or three prophets should speak" (1 Cor. 14:29).
8. Others must weigh carefully what the prophets say (1 Cor. 14:29).

9. "And if a revelation comes to someone who is sitting down, the first speaker should stop" (1 Cor. 14:30).
10. Each person can prophesy in turn "so that everyone may be instructed and encouraged" (1 Cor. 14:31).
11. "[D]o not forbid speaking in tongues" (1 Cor. 14:39).
12. Do everything "in a fitting and orderly way" (1 Cor. 14:40).

Paul's other desires:

- "I would like every one of you to speak in tongues" (1 Cor. 14:5).
- "I would rather have you prophesy. He who prophesies is greater than one who speaks in tongues, unless he interprets" (1 Cor. 14:5).
- "[T]ry to excel in gifts that build up the church" (1 Cor. 14:12).

This Week

- In your prayers, eagerly desire the gift of prophecy for the strengthening, encouragement and comfort of those around you. Especially desire words from the Spirit of God as you speak to your children, your grandchildren and those God brings into your sphere of influence.

- God may bring you someone you don't know well and give you the words of wisdom or knowledge or prophecy to help them find the kingdom of God—to keep them safe from the evil one and away from harm. Pray that He reveals someone in whom He's working and whom He wants you to come alongside.

- God has given you a gift or gifts with which to tend and take care of the part of the world in which you walk. If you want more or if you want to seek out His will for you today and in the last days of your life, ask Him if He has more of them to give you at this time in your life. And, as Paul suggests, "[T]ry to excel in gifts that build up the church" (1 Cor. 14:12) and in those that advance the kingdom of God.

- The gift of discerning between spirits is something I needed at times in my life. I needed someone with this gift to keep myself and others from harm. Use this gift if you have it, and listen to those who have it, before you trust someone you don't know well and allow them influence over you and others.

"When I was a child, I talked like a child, I thought like a child, I reasoned like a child. When I became a man, I put childish ways behind me. Now we see but a poor reflection as in a mirror; then we shall see face to face. Now I know in part; then I shall know fully, even as I am fully known. And now these three remain: faith, hope and love. But the greatest of these is love (1 Cor. 13:11–13)."

. . . .

"Surely," we will be bold . . .

Some time ago a couple arrived for their gifted vacation at a beautiful resort by the sea. Many of their friends had told them about this heaven on earth, the crystal pools with exquisite fish swirling like a rainbow of mystical colors that danced for them when snorkeling, the white sands easy to enjoy the sun from, the tropical birds flying among the palm trees. Their room overlooked the early rising sun across the waters. The moon danced its light to them across the evening waves as they stood on their balcony. From sand to room to sea to food delights and more, their life was made perfect in this resort by the shore.

Upon their return, life renewed, and they thought to tell each person they knew of the treasures and gifts given in this place by the sea, and how they could be better, happier—even free.

We will be strong in our spirits and in the grace and love that is in Christ Jesus. In our freedom, we will flame the gift within us, and testify of our Lord with our words and with our lives.

[F]an into flame the Gift of God which is in you . . . For God did not give us a spirit of timidity, but a spirit of power, of love and of self-discipline. So, do not be ashamed to testify about our Lord. (2 Tim. 1:6-8)

17

DON'T BE ASHAMED TO TESTIFY ABOUT JESUS

Have you ever received a gift, perhaps at Christmas, and just put it away and forgot you received it? Maybe you missed its significance, its importance, its benefit to you or meaning in your life.

Sometimes we have gifts around us we take for granted—like people. We don't engage with them. We don't pay attention to them. At times, we don't even see them. Without thinking about it, in many ways we take them for granted.

We may say to each other, "Good morning. How are you?"

"Fine, thank you. How are you?"

We say the words, go through the unavoidable moment but we're not present—not really. This even happens in significant relationships.

I sit here at my desk thinking about my mother. As the oldest child, I was spoiled by her and my dad, and I'm grateful for it, but missed seeing them at times, seeing the best of them, seeing their concern for me and seeing their support for me. Today, I miss them. I miss being with them.

Do you have someone you miss? I pray you tell them you miss them, even if they're gone. I pray you do this today.

Jesus and the Father love you. Their death and resurrection prove this is true.

Remember the last words of JJ Heller's song assure us Jesus will give us the love—the love we never knew. To strengthen their lyrics and your faith, hold onto this promise of Jesus:

> For God so loved the world that he gave his one and only Son, that whoever believes in him shall not perish but have eternal life. For God did not send his Son into the world to condemn the world, but to save the world through him. (John 3:16–17)

JJ tells us about the kid alone in the corner, the woman whose husband leaves her and the prisoner who cries out to God.

What's your story? Is it the woman at the well, the rich young man, Mary Magdalene, Hannah or the thief on the cross? Is it the story of the privileged firstborn, or the forgotten kid on the play yard? Are you the middle child or the one bullied in the play yard?

Are you the parent with a child you cannot help? Did you grow up without a home or did you live as a child with parents who loved you? Did you have to squeeze a penny or was money plentiful around you? Are you grateful for someone?

Do you understand and experience in your spirit the low position of your riches and the high position of the poor? Do you know that the king and the pauper go into the same box after the chess game ends and life stops?

Do you feel forgiven? Do you feel saved by the truth and the work of His Son, Jesus? Do you know you are God's child— His prince or princess? Have you been tempted or led into situations that later caused you to doubt God's love for you?

Did you spend your early years trying to earn the favor of an earthly father? Do you feel you fall short now doing the same for your heavenly one?

Alone, discarded and condemned. This is who we were before Christ.

He redeemed us. He saved us. He is our peace and our hope and our joy. He is risen. We *are* children of God. We walk in the light and out of the darkness because of the King of kings, the lamb of God. We have His amazing grace.

Praise be to the God and Father of our Lord Jesus Christ, the Father of compassion and the God of all comfort, *who comforts us in all our troubles, so that we can comfort those in any trouble with the comfort we ourselves have received from God.* For just as the sufferings of Christ flow over into our lives, so also through Christ our comfort overflows. (2 Cor. 1:3–5)

He is . . .

(Please say these out loud as you pray to God and deepen your gratefulness for Him!)

He is who He is (Ex. 3:14).

He is to be remembered through all generations (Ex. 4:9).

He is the Lord my healer (Ex. 15:26).

He is compassionate (Ex. 22:27).

He is the Lord who sanctifies me (Lev. 22:32).

He is the Lord my God (1 Chr. 16:14).

He is good (1 Chr. 16:34).

He is a holy God (Josh. 24:19).

He is a jealous God (Josh. 24:19).

He is a shield for all those who take refuge in Him (2 Sam 22:31).

He is the saving refuge of His anointed (Psa. 28:8).

He is God Almighty (Gen. 35:11).

He is great in power (Job 37:23).

He is the King of glory (Psa. 24:10).

He is my help and my shield (Psa. 33:20).

He is my stronghold in times of trouble (Psa. 37:39).

He is highly exalted (Psa. 47:9).

He is awesome in His deeds toward the children of men (Psa. 66:5).

He is the one who gives power and strength to his people (Psa. 68:35).

He is my rock (Psa. 92:15).

He is robed in majesty (Psa. 93:1).

He is gracious, merciful and righteous (Psa. 112:4).

He is the true God (Jer. 10:10).

He is the living God and the everlasting King (Jer. 10:10).

He is the one who formed all things (Jer. 10:16).

He is gracious and merciful (Joel 2:13).

He is slow to anger, abounding in steadfast love (Joel 2:13).

He is my great reward (Gen. 15:1).

He is gentle and lowly in heart (Matt. 11:29).

He is with me always, to the end of the age (Matt. 28:20).

He is the Word, the Logos (John 1:1).

He is the bread of life (John 6:48).

He is the light of the world (John 8:12).

He is the gate for the sheep. He is the good shepherd (John 10:7, 11).

He is the resurrection and the life (John 11:25).

He is the true vine (John 15:1).

He is the Alpha and the Omega—the beginning and the end (Rev. 1:8).

He is the first and the last (Rev. 1:17).

He is making all things new (Rev. 21:5).

He is the bright Morning Star (Rev. 22:16).

He is Jesus.

He is the Holy Spirit.

He is God.

If anyone loves God, he "is known by God" (1 Cor. 8:3).

"Therefore, if anyone is in Christ, he is a new creation" (2 Cor. 5:17).

Who I am in Christ . . .

I am a friend of Jesus Christ (Rom. 15:15).

I have been justified (declared righteous) (Rom. 5:1).

I am united with the Lord, and I am one with Him in spirit (1 Cor. 6:17).

I have been bought with a price and I belong to God (1 Cor. 6:19–20).

I am a member of Christ's body (1 Cor. 12:27).

I have been chosen by God and adopted as His child (Eph. 1:3–8).

I have been redeemed and forgiven of all sins (Col. 1:13–14).

I am complete in Christ (Col. 2:9–10).

I have direct access to the throne of grace through Christ Jesus (Heb. 4:14–16).

I am free of condemnation (Rom. 8:1).

I am assured that God works for my good in all circumstances (Rom. 8:28).

I am a citizen of heaven (Phil. 3:20).

I have been given a spirit of power, love and a sound mind (2 Tim. 1:7).

I am born of God and the evil one cannot touch me (1 John 5:18).

I am God's temple (1 Cor. 3:16).

I am God's workmanship (Eph. 2:10).

I may approach God with freedom and confidence (Eph. 3:12).

I can do all things through Christ, who strengthens me (Phil. 4:13).

I am born again (1 Peter 1:23).

I am a child of God (John 1:12; 1 John 3:1–2, 10; 5:19).

Testify About Jesus: Filled with the Holy Spirit

When we read about the saints of old, each time someone is "filled with the Holy Spirit," they are enabled and empowered to testify boldly about Jesus—His coming, His death and resurrection and the good news of the gospel. This occurs with Elizabeth (Luke 1:41), Zechariah (Luke 1:67), Peter on the day of Pentecost (Acts 2), Peter and John with the Sanhedrin council (Acts 4:8) and with Paul as he testifies across the world in synagogues and to the Gentiles (Acts 9:17; 13:9, 12).

When the disciples were filled with joy and the Holy Spirit, they spoke with great effectiveness and many believed in Jesus (Acts 13:52; 14:1). That's what we want as well—to be filled with the Holy Spirit for those moments he brings someone to us. We want to be ready and willing for His use in the salvation of a lost soul or a brother or sister needing an increase in their faith.

Even in times of turmoil, persecution and godless chatter in the world, Paul writes:

> For this reason I remind you to *fan into flame* the gift of God, which is in you through the laying on of my hands. For God did not give us a spirit of timidity, but a spirit of power, of love and of self-discipline. *So do not be ashamed to testify about our Lord.* (2 Tim. 1:6–8)

As Paul suffers and is imprisoned in chains, he reminds young Timothy, who is like a son to him, to overcome an attack upon his faith. He asks him to rekindle his gift, fan it into a flame, to endure hardship and to do the work of an evangelist.

The Greek verb for "testify" Paul uses here comes from the Greek noun **μαρτυς** (*martys*), meaning "to witness." It's used 34 times in the New Testament. Paul wants Timothy witnessing to others just as his grandmother Lois and his mother Eunice did for him out of their sincere faith.

When we walk in the Spirit, we can hear the very voice of God and "The Spirit himself testifies with our spirit that we are God's children" (Rom. 8:16). Because of His love in our lives, we pray to be used by Him to bring others into the grace of Jesus. Then our hearts and our senses, guided by a sincere faith and love for Jesus, will know when the Spirit brings someone to us to hear our testimony.

God may want us to talk with a child in our family or a brother or sister in Christ struggling with their faith. He may bring someone to us at church or at work, at home or during a vacation.

Each day we pray for our gift of Christ to spread from the Spirit within us. That's why it's so important for us to allow the discipline and training of God upon our lives. We're living testimonies and ambassadors of Christ wherever we go.

As we walk through life in the Spirit, He changes us into the likeness of Christ. *He gives us a redemptive story*, and God wants us ready and willing to share it with power, love and a sound mind.

DON'T BE ASHAMED TO TESTIFY ABOUT JESUS

Hear, O Israel: The Lord our God, the Lord is one. Love the Lord your God with all your heart and with all your soul and with all your strength. *These commandments that I give you today are to be upon your hearts. Impress them on your children. Talk about them when you sit at home and when you walk along the road, when you lie down and when you get up. Tie them as symbols on your hands and bind them on your foreheads. Write them on the door frames of your houses and on your gates.* (Deut. 6:4–9)

When the Counselor comes, whom I will send to you from the Father, the Spirit of truth who goes out from the Father, he will testify about me. *And you also must testify, for you have been with me from the beginning.* (John 15:26–27)

We share stories all the time. We talk about experiences and what they mean to us. When we do, we often talk about the impact these things have on our lives—how they helped us, changed our mind or impacted our emotional well-being. This includes both the negative and positive things we encounter.

If God wants us to tell someone about Jesus, this means He knows our personal story of transformation will help them. He wants us to be ready for the moment and the person He brings to us. He wants us in faith to be courageous.

The following night the Lord stood near Paul and said, "Take courage! *As you have testified about me in Jerusalem, so you must also testify in Rome.*" (Acts 23:11)

However, I consider my life worth nothing to me, if only I may finish the race and complete the task the Lord Jesus has given me—*the task of testifying to the gospel of God's grace.* (Acts 20:24)

As the Spirit moves you, tell the person He brings you what was going on in your life when you were not in God's will—how you harmed yourself or others by what you did. Tell the person about your life before you found Jesus. Then, tell them about the struggle, the change, and the disciplining process you experienced until finally peace entered your life where before you couldn't find it.

After you gave your life to Jesus as your Lord and savior, tell them about the difference He made in your heart and in your life. Explain how he now walks with and leads you by the Spirit of God.

Each person God brings you will have a story. You may pray with some. To others you may lend a hand or serve them in some way. As you pray and as you walk with each, whether a believer or not, be sensitive to the Spirit's leading.

It's His timing you want—not yours. It's His words you want—not yours. It's His testimony about Jesus you want—not yours. Talking to others about Jesus in your life or theirs is not about eloquence or superior wisdom, but weakness and fear and trembling. You have what it takes, and He is Jesus. His Spirit is in you.

Be confident, in Him.

Be thoughtful, in Him.

Be loving toward each person He brings to you, in Him.

Be prayerful in the Spirit toward each word you say and each action you take.

This Week

- Look each day for whom God wants you to come alongside and help with a word of strengthening, encouragement or comfort. Work to fan the flame of faith within you. Look for those who will help you see the love of God in your life. Grow in His grace—the knowledge of your identity in Christ Jesus.

- You do still sin. That's true. He's winning victories within you through the changing power of His Spirit. That's true. Your identity, whether you feel this is true or not, is this: "You are a dearly loved child of God." That's true! Memorize and meditate upon the "He is" and "I am" verses and clean the muddy lens of untruth from your sight. You are a born-again new creation of God. That's true! To bring the good news to the world around you, firmly rest in the peace of your salvation and the love of God.

- All of us testify about Jesus and our love for Him. We do this every day with our behavior and words. We make a remarkable difference in the lives of those we touch. We serve them. We pray with them and, when He prompts us, we testify and tell our stories about Jesus. We do this in the Spirit and with the Spirit. We do nothing on our own and He supplies us with what we need for His purposes as He advances the kingdom of God through the Spirit within us. We are His lights in the world!

When I came to you, brothers, I did not come with eloquence or superior wisdom as I proclaimed to you the testimony about God. For I resolved to know nothing while I was with you except Jesus Christ and him crucified. I came to you in weakness and fear, and with much trembling. My message and my preaching were not with wise and persuasive words, but with a demonstration of the Spirit's power, so that your faith might not rest on men's wisdom, but on God's power. (1 Cor. 2:1–5)

. . . .

the sharing of a better dream . . .

A man long ago dreamed up a business to help people help people. It was a business of good food placed in tablets for better health. Even physicians joined this business and liked the idea of better health through better diets made easy by pills. Many users of this product sang its benefits and became impassioned advocates who "shared" it with others, who "shared" it with others, who "shared" it with others . . . Everyone "shared" in the profits as well. The spirt of this enterprise ran through its people.

What is the spirt within you living for? Easy pills for and easy life? What do you share with those around you? Who or what is your rock?

For through him [Jesus] we both [Jewish and Gentile Christians] have access to the Father by one Spirit.

Consequently, you are no longer foreigners and aliens, but fellow citizens with God's people and members of God's household, built on the foundation of the apostles and prophets, with Christ Jesus himself as the chief cornerstone. (Eph. 2:18–20)

18

A NEW PERSON: A NEW FAMILY (REVIVAL)

He hovers over the waters
and waits
for God to speak
light into the world!

See, I am doing a new thing!
—a new thing in you
Now up it springs
do you not perceive it? (Is. 43:19)

I am making a way in the desert
—streams in the wasteland (Is. 43:19)
I am the Spirit
do you not see it?

I am releasing you from laws
—in the new way of the Spirit (Rom. 7:6)
My name is Jesus
do you not love me?

I am giving you a new heart
—a new spirit in you
I am removing your heart of stone
do you not know it (Ezek. 36:26)

I am not writing you
a new command
but one you had from the beginning
Love one another (John 13:34; 1 John 2:7–8; 2 John 5)

*I*n this broken world, chaos reigns over order. Fractures appear. They begin to happen in all things at the moment of their creation. Even a chair in a corner begins to break down over time. The natural randomness of unguided molecules and gravity begin to tear it apart. Therefore, a room or a life without attention becomes messy.

If in darkness, the disorder or deterioration can accelerate because it's more difficult to organize and repair what's hidden in the dark. Sometimes you cannot see the mess or what hides in the shadows of its gloomy covering.

That's why sin and evil increase at night. Without light, it is harder to detect them. A darkened room, a dimly lit bar or a night without a moon—these darkened conditions make it tough to keep things right and easier to cause or do mischief.

We're genetically predisposed to sin—to oppose light, to do wrong. Without the Spirit of God within us, without His personal presence, we tend toward making things worse by our own efforts. We worry, criticize, fight, gossip, act without gentleness, become impatient, lose control of ourselves, go off on our own, compete with one another or sit in the corner when people need help. We make things worse. We tend to arrange things so we take care of our own needs and desires. We sin.

It is even easier for us to sin when our consciences darken and our hearts harden. Vulnerability to sin increases as we separate ourselves from the life of God in us. We lose sensitivity to sin. Paul explains the deteriorating path to sin in this way:

> They are darkened in their understanding and *separated from the life of God* because of the ignorance that is in them due to the hardening of their hearts. Having lost all sensitivity, they have given themselves over to sensuality so as to indulge in every kind of impurity, with a continual lust for more. (Eph. 4:18–19)

Years ago, I remember a brother in Christ talking about his personality and bad behavior toward another person. With a cynical tone, he said, "That's just who I am!" Perhaps, I heard him wrongly, but at the time I heard an excuse for his rudeness or lack of sensitivity. I also learned the reason for his spiritual world view. He believed in a god (little "g") who is uninvolved in our lives—who got the world spinning and now just watches.

I couldn't live a Spiritless life with an impersonal god and an unchanging me. My family couldn't either. Growing up, I had lived with an impersonal and increasingly remote father due to his alcohol dependency. I needed to believe that God, our heavenly Father, not only cared, but wanted to walk through life with us.

I wanted to believe He'd give me strength and wisdom. I wanted to believe He'd be with me. I wanted to believe He'd die for me. I wanted to believe in the good news. I wanted to believe in Jesus.

Before Christ, we doom ourselves to lives of unchanging desperation and hopelessness. To cope with this messed-up world and our broken and sin-filled condition, we become cynics, abusers, workaholics or hedonistic idol-worshiping people. We trust the futility of our thinking and the objects of our impulses.

To stop the cycle of falling into the same temptations, we need a miracle. *We need the living presence of God within us.* We need Him to walk with us each day. We need the faith, hope and love of God active in our lives. We need His transformation.

A New Way, a New Person, a New Life

When we believe in Jesus, we receive the Spirit of God and we are baptized into a new life (Gal. 3:2; Acts 2:38). Though we cannot see Him, He does a grace-filled and new thing in us. He makes us better people—people of God with reborn spirits alive in righteousness. (Rom. 8:10)

He chisels away and removes our hearts of stone. He connects with and brings our spirits back to life. Streams of living water spring up within our hearts and begin to heal and move away the former wasteland of sinful habits and evil tendencies.

As He works in us, and as we walk in the Spirit with prayer and in His will, He frees us from the bondage of sin one victory at a time. People who know us can see the changes occurring. They can see the miracle of God within us. They experience our kindness and gentleness toward them. They experience our patience with them. They see our joy and our steadfast and sacrificial love even in difficult circumstances. They see the gifts of the Spirt and know we're of God. "And we, who with unveiled faces all reflect the Lord's glory, are *being transformed into his likeness with ever-increasing glory, which comes from the Lord, who is the Spirit*" (2 Cor. 3:18).

This is true. No matter how we feel or how we mess up in life, this is true. The Spirit gives us a new birth—not from the womb, but from God. We are born of and by the Spirit into our new life. Therefore, we don't set aside the grace of God and attempt to attain righteousness through our own efforts. We don't make Christ's death of no effect. We don't live foolishly without His Spirit and without His gifts. We die with Jesus and submit to the Spirit of God.

We walk each day as new creations in a new life with miracles working among us. With our new spiritual powers and our new family, we put off and repel the old self and its corruption and deceitful desires. With prayer, fasting, gifts of the Spirit and devotion to God, we fulfill His new command. We love each other and the people on this earth. We put on our new selves, which from the beginning were created to be like God in true righteousness and holiness (Eph. 4:24).

A New Family: Joined in Christ

Those in the world who confess with their mouths and say, "Jesus is Lord" and believe in their hearts that God raised Him from the dead will be saved (Rom. 10:9). Paul tells us that "no one who is speaking by the Spirit of God says, 'Jesus be cursed,'" and "no one can say, 'Jesus is Lord,' except by the Holy Spirit" (1 Cor. 12:3). Those who do believe in Christ "have access to the Father by one Spirit" (Eph. 2:18).

No matter our earthly family and its origins and allegiances, no matter the churches we attended as children, before Christ, we live without hope and without God. We exist separated and excluded from citizenship in heaven and foreigners to the covenants of the promise, until that day—the day that we enter God's household by the blood of Christ. In our new family, we find ourselves in the presence of the Father by one Spirit and join fellow citizens, God's people, everywhere. In Him, we join together and rise as a holy temple in the Lord to advance the kingdom of God (Eph. 2:1–21).

Our new family looks like an earthly family except it has a superpower within it—the Spirit of God. All of us receive different gifts from Him, and eagerly seek more to use for the manifestation of the common good. The same Spirit joins us together as we build the body up in love—each part doing its work (Eph. 4:16).

We walk with each other in our struggles and pray for each other in the Spirit on all occasions. We always keep on praying for all the saints (Eph. 6:18).

We know the end of all things is near. We clear our minds and allow the Spirit to control us so we can pray—remembering to love each person deeply, for love covers a multitude of sins. We offer each other hospitality without grumbling and use whatever gift we receive to serve others—faithfully administering God's grace in a variety of ways at home, at work and as we live out each day. We speak as though speaking the very words of God. We serve with the strength the Father supplies so that in all things He may be praised through Jesus Christ (paraphrase of 1 Pet. 4:7–11).

In Him, we advance like a stream of holy water moving across the planet watering it and bringing spiritual nutrients. We do good to all people, all races, in all countries, of all social and economic means, to everyone, and we especially love those who "belong to the family of believers" (Gal. 6:10).

Do we need to remember our first love? Do we need the love of Christ in our hearts? Do we need to love each saint we meet in every corner of the world? Do we need revival? Lord revive us—revive the Spirit within us!

This Week

- Ask yourself, "Does God need to do a new thing in me?" Ask God in prayer, "Do you need to do a new thing in me?"

- Do you see chaos in your life or the life of your family? Is there any nagging area of messiness that you want to submit to God? Are you willing to allow Him in to heal you in this area? Or, are you resigned to the carnal mindset "That's just the way I am"? Please realize that if you are, then this unspiritual attitude will also extend to your children, your friends, the people and world around you. It will make you hopeless, depressed, angry, full of excuses or a person of gossip. This spirit will render you useless for the work of God.

- Do you live with a deist perspective—one that includes the belief that God made the world, gave it a great big spin, and now watches to see what happens? Do you believe that the Spirit is active in your life? Can we see this in your home? Is God displayed on its doorposts? Is it a house of prayer? Are you a house of prayer? Is your church family a house of prayer?

- Are you one in the Spirit with brothers and sisters who have given their lives to Jesus Christ throughout the world? Do you pray for all the saints within your present church family and within the other church families across the world? We're all in the body of Christ. We're one stream of conquerors.

Now we have access to the Father by one Spirit and *are fellow citizens with God's people* everywhere. In Him, we're joined together and rise as a holy temple in the Lord to advance the kingdom of God.

. . . .

asking the right source . . .

A general once asked himself, "What will win this war? Will it be the tanks, or the soldiers, or the planes, or the bombs?" Then, he thought, "How can we surprise the enemy and win? What gift can we give them—what will be our Trojan Horse?"

Businesses think in the same way, "What gift can we give our customers—how can we get to know them, and how can they get to know us?" or, "What can we do that will help them see we're cost effective and good for them?"

The leaders of companies and armies open themselves up to what will help them advance—what will help them win. They're shrewd. They're intense. They're creative when the times demand something new—something more effective than the weapons or tools of a time long ago.

The Spirit of God is the creative intelligence who hovered over the dark void in the beginning. He is the Spirit of "The Great I Am." He always knows what to do—the when, the how and the where for bringing Jesus to those who are lost, to those who need their lives transformed. Ask Him and do what He says.

To the weak I became weak, to win the weak. I have become all things to all men so that by all possible means I might save some. (1 Cor. 9:22)

19

A NEW CHURCH:
A COMMUNITY (REVIVAL)

When people think of a poodle, they think it has a French origin with its hair cut by a stylist into various, and sometimes amazing, styles. They see it as an intelligent performer at circuses—a dog of various colors and sizes performing tricks for an audience. Poodle owners are stereotyped as people of means who enjoy having a "show" poodle on a leash accompany them.

However, most researchers believe the poodle originated in Germany and weighs as much as 70 pounds, with a height of 24 inches to the shoulder. Its name derives from German, *Pudel*, which means "to splash." It was Germany's water dog, very athletic and intelligent as a trained hunting dog for ducks, geese and other waterfowl.

If it senses danger, it quickly protects its master or family. Since at least the seventeenth century, hunting Poodles were used as working dogs in the military and were easily trained to ignore gunfire. In World War II, "The men were initially skeptical of 'the 'exotic breeds,' particularly the Poodles, but these men soon learned that even such 'Park Avenue' pets were he-men at heart," reported the *Saturday Evening Post* (September 5, 1942).

One famous poodle, "Moustache," was a pet of French soldiers and a part of the Napoleonic wars. He famously sniffed out an Austrian spy and saved his platoon of soldiers from an enemy attack. Once, when a soldier died while attempting to save the flag by wrapping it around his body, "Moustache" retrieved the flag by working to unwrap it. He carried it back to his own lines in victory. When introduced to Napoleon, he performed various tricks including his most famous, the lifting of his leg at the mention of the enemy's name. For saving the flag he was given a tricolor collar to wear with a silver medal, engraved "Moustache, A French dog, a brave fighter entitled to respect—At the Battle of Austerlitz, he had his leg broken while saving the flag of his regiment." After accompanying his soldiers back into battle, he died from a cannon ball. His burial stone simply says, *Ci gît le brave Moustache*. Now, that's a poodle!

People Who Love Jesus and One Another

People don't picture poodles in the military. Why? Why do you picture a church in a building? Why does its definition have to include a building? Our culture stereotypes worship places and the believers who meet there. Is it possible that this stereotype could impede the gifts and work of the Spirit in our present-day culture? Why or why not?

Describe a first-century church and its people. Where do they meet? Why? What do they do? Who leads them? Why do they grow? How are they similar to today's fast-growing churches in China?

Did you know the Quakers did not call their meeting place a church; instead, they called it a steeplehouse? For the sake of purity, they didn't want to refer to a building as a church because the church was a spiritual community.

Believers in America meet in a building where one person speaks to them each week. They sit looking straight ahead at him. Often by themselves and at times not connecting with anyone around them, they leave for home alone. They meet in a place where one hundred or five thousand or more people sit in front-facing rows and listen to someone's prepared lesson. They sing or listen to familiar songs. They sit in the same places and see other believers once or twice a week. Why wouldn't that model work in the first century or in China?

Hundreds of years before the first century, people gathered in a circle around a fire for celebration and worship and protection. In this intimate setting, with those they knew well, they gathered and told stories.

As their crowds became larger and tribes turned into cities, their stories turned into theater. Performances moved from being in-the-round, to outdoor stages. In the fifth century BC, these were set at the bottom of Grecian hills where the people sat, in rows facing down and forward. Many could watch the plays while looking down on the actors and actresses. Later, their plays were moved indoors and became the future seating arrangement for buildings used by believers in the third century. Today, the theater calls this less intimate arrangement of hundreds of people a proscenium-arranged stage. This arrangement has become suitable for the stereotypical church.

Imagine people in a large country with multiple idols and many choices where to place their worship. They carry or display some graven form of their spiritual attention, and the politicians control the country's acceptance of certain higher-ordered gods. Ancestors are prayed to as well.

Sexual promiscuity and orientations of all types are a celebrated part of life. Common practice allows marriages to contain liaisons with people other than those whom they married. Orgies are normal.

The rich and poor live apart and in very different conditions. A mother abandons her unwanted child. As the child grows, it is subject to being raped. The Bible does not exist. The person and name of Jesus is unknown.

With most of the world under Roman rule, a carpenter known as a leader of a weird new sect becomes very unpopular with Jewish religious leaders—so unpopular that they demand the Roman governor crucify Him with common criminals. This happens and Jesus, who claims He is the Son of God, and King of the Jews, dies on a cross between two other accused men.

After His death, this sect and new religion rises and begins to grow amidst severe persecution. It teaches marriage for life, one man and one woman. It teaches that sexual union confines itself to those within a marriage. Children are celebrated and protected. It lifts up the poor and sick and cares for them. It lowers the position of the rich. Women and men are equally loved and valued.

The people of this socially radical sect meet in homes and grow in number. This happens even though the day's religious and political leaders stone or throw the new sect's followers to lions, who tear them apart in gladiator arenas. These enemies drag them from their homes and murder or burn them—but growth continues.

Yet, in three hundred years and under an extended holocaust of many believers, according to some estimates 10 percent of the Roman empire becomes Christian and the story of Jesus is spread from house to house across much of the world. Why? How did this happen without military or political force or buildings or tradition?

Those early Christians did nothing in their own effort. They prayed and lived each day holding onto their faith and experiencing the hope and love of God. They trusted in Jesus and in the Spirit and in receiving all the gifts, power, truth and comfort He provides.

Fast forward to China and the twenty-first century. Government workers complete the demolition of a large church building while small bands of believers watch. The police block a road to keep people from an escape to the mountains. They cut off power to the whole area and black out mobile coverage. They try to stop anyone from coming near the huge building about to collapse.

It is April 28, 2014. These actions begin the launch of a very visible campaign to stop the fastest-growth "foreign" religion in this atheist-ordered country. This building is just a part of an "official church" built by the approved branch of the government and is torn down as a demonstration of government power. The *Financial Times* reports, "Hundreds of people have been detained for short periods and some remain in custody, accused under ambiguous crimes more often used to punish political dissidents." Many Christians just disappear.

The Chinese political and socialist authorities call religion the "opiate of the masses." And yet at its current pace of growth, China will become the world's largest Christian population within 15 years. Nearly all of its growth will occur in the homes of the Chinese people and not in a building like the one the government collapsed. Today, it is estimated that 100 million Christians reside in China.

For centuries, Christianity surged and dropped back, but continued to fight its way into China. In the late 1980s, the Christians there were rural, uneducated females and elderly. Eight out of ten of them lived in poor areas.

In these times, amidst rampant consumerism, cynicism and materialism, a lack of idealism or ethics exists in modern Chinese society. Cultural shifts include observable sexual diversity (homosexual and bisexual behavior), internet sex, a separation of sex from love and child-bearing and a separation of sex from marriage. China also faces a growing problem of illicit drug use that is expanding at an unprecedented speed. This describes the social setting that exists amidst humanism, secularism, Buddhism, Taoism and Islam along with the exponential growth of Christianity.

Tens of millions of Chinese Christians attend underground "house churches" not recognized or approved by the state. These increase daily. Why? How did this happen without social power or buildings or tradition?

The Chinese believers do nothing in their own effort. Like the early Christians in fear for their lives, they pray and live each day holding onto their faith and experiencing the hope and love of God. They trust in Jesus and in the Spirit and in receiving all the gifts, power, truth and comfort He provides.

When things are safe outside and life is easy to live, those who believe in Christ can lose their first love and ambition to see the kingdom of God advance in themselves and others. They walk in their own effort and without the Spirit. They don't see the dangers of an immoral society even when they become plain for those who look with honest reflection. Lukewarm hearts blind their ability to see the effects upon the people outside their church buildings or homes. They may find themselves supporting the killing of babies or infants or the elderly because of "the freedom to choose." They may not care to discuss sexuality with their children and instead allow them "to find their own way." Facing the front, they attend church in a building once a week, and do not see or care for the pain of others near them. They may live with the same sins or even allow sex to be paraded in front of their eyes at a movie theater or in the privacy of their home as they watch television.

However, when fearful, courageous people, in solidarity against the forces opposing them, sit together in a home and pray in the Spirit, something of great significance happens. In the presence of a fallen world and among people skeptical of their convictions, God strengthens, encourages and comforts them. They have everything in common. They eat together with sincere and glad hearts. They praise God. They enjoy the favor of people in need because they pray for them, care for them and teach them about Jesus and the good news of His presence in their lives. They study together and prepare together for the days ahead. They use their spiritual gifts for the common good and see miracles happen in the lives of others. They teach others about Jesus and disciple them. If the Lord wills, He adds daily those who are being saved.

As American society follows Roman and Chinese societies into secularism, how can we use our homes, workplaces and other gathering places for the advancement of the kingdom? How can we speak into the culture and fight the powers and principalities organizing the political and social forces around us?

With the help of the Spirit of God alone, and not our own efforts, we fight with divine weapons. We do this as we trust in the Spirit, and He wins others to Christ and the number of the saved increases.

A Family of Believers Led by the Spirit of God

Our church is not a building. We, the church, are children of God who believe in the saving work of Jesus Christ. We submit everything we do or possess to Him every day and live in faith. This means every ministry we begin, or within which we work, is led by the Spirit of God. He is our counselor, through prayer, and nothing is decided or done in our own effort.

Within our body exists people with various gifts. Our elders, when and if they are appointed, shepherd us in prayer and in truth and lead us in the Spirit. All of us receive our direction and power in prayer and from the Spirit of God.

We use our Spirit-given gifts for the common good. We're a witness to everyone, and remember that Jesus said His house is a "house of prayer," not of preaching, teaching, singing or anything else—but first a house of prayer.

Healings occur among us spiritually, emotionally and physically. These occur because we submit what comes against us and against those around us to the Spirit's power. We confess our needs and temptations and weaknesses to one another and pray for one another—even with groans that words cannot express.

We listen to God and eagerly seek the gift of prophecy. We speak prophetic words that strengthen, encourage and comfort one another. We do this to make all of us better and to serve and love one another and those within the world around us.

Whether we use a house or a building, or if we go to a retirement home or to a cabin or to the inner city, our journey and work are motivated and accomplished by the Spirit within us. We do everything to advance the kingdom of God in each other, in our families and in those parts of the earth to which the Spirit prompts us to go.

For example, the Spirit may lead us to open a coffee shop or a restaurant, or a golf course or a home for kids and find ways to bring Christ to anyone who enters and enjoys their time there. Those the Spirit brings to these places may see the words "love," "joy," "peace," "patience," "kindness," "goodness," "faithfulness," "gentleness" and "self-control" written across the tops of the walls in the bathrooms. The people who serve there do so with a welcoming grace and smiles of hospitality, and often find themselves in spiritual conversations with their customers.

The Spirit may lead someone to the inner city to bring practical help and love and Bibles and prayer. Others find themselves moved to come with food alongside those in need. Some offer teaching gifts. A few look for moments to offer salvation and all find themselves unified in the work of the Spirit.

The Spirit moves us at home and at work. He comforts us in our hearts or through the hugs and words of our brothers and sisters. He convicts us of sin. He gives us the ability to forgive the unforgivable and takes away our judgement. He works on our hearts and personalities and over time changes us into better people—people who are more Christlike wherever we go. Christian attorneys and bricklayers, engineers and secretaries, hair stylists and athletes, moms and dads—they all do what they do in the world to serve and bring others to Jesus.

We pray unceasingly for this guidance as we wake up and as we lie down. All of our different gifts and prophetic abilities and interpretations of Scripture bring spiritual thoughts and movements of God that help each of us live a life of love. As a church body, we're made up of individuals who are one in Christ Jesus. We're made as imagers of God.

At just the right time, the Spirit of God shows some of us "a certain way" to bring Jesus and the word of God to those who need Him in this present-day world. When the Spirit moves these people to begin, others with different gifts and talents join them in the place where God is working.

While all us seek the gift of evangelism for those God brings to us, others know they are evangelists and spread the gospel as a full-time ministry. While we all seek the gift of prophecy for specific moments, some seem to have this gift most of the time. However, when we listen to anyone who offers a word from God, we test those words to see if they are true and from the Spirit.

As the times change, families of believers may be led to alter how they approach the world. In this new way, they bring people to Jesus and serve them in the way the Spirit leads. As changed people, linked by the Spirit to other families of believers, they live as ambassadors of Christ and bring God's rule to the world one person at a time. They live transformed lives in the Spirit of God.

Accept the call upon your heart and give your life to Jesus—for real. The Spirit will live within you and bring you a full life—maybe not a perfect one—maybe not an easy one—but a purposeful one that will bring rest to your soul.

God loves you and wants you with Him always.

This Week

- We know the Greek work used in the Bible for the English word church was **εκκλησια** (*ekklēsia*), from *ek*, "out from and to" and *kaleō*, "to call," people called out from the world and to God and His Son and to His ministry in the Spirit—Christians striving together to advance the kingdom of God. Sometimes previous and accepted social norms and appearances keep us from seeing how to identify a poodle or a church according to its real makeup and purpose. So, how can present-day church form and tradition keep us from seeing our mission—keep us from growing—keep us from using our gifts for the benefit of our brothers and sisters and those still "in the world?"

- Why do you think the Quakers didn't want to call their building a church? What were they trying to avoid? Why did it matter—isn't this just semantics?

- Have you experienced worship in an intimate setting within your home or the home of someone else? Why do you think this intimacy exists there in a way different from the corporate facing-front seating of the typical church building? Does intimacy also diminish as the number of people grows larger?

- How are the individual gifts of the Spirit magnified in a close community? Why do we need to display them among us when we come together?

All the believers were together and had everything in common. Selling their possessions and goods, they gave to anyone as he had need. Every day they continued to meet together in the temple courts. They broke bread in their homes and ate together with glad and sincere hearts, praising God and enjoying the favor of all the people. And the Lord added to their number daily those who were being saved. (Acts 2:44–47)

. . . .

what we seek we find . . .

The father eagerly awaits his son back from the war. The student eagerly awaits the posting of his grades. The couple eagerly awaits the arrival of their child. The patient eagerly awaits the passing of his illness. The coach and his team eagerly await the beginning of the season. Those who are hungry eagerly await a meal. The family eagerly awaits the completion of their home. The bride and groom eagerly await their marriage.

Where hope remains, and faith strengthens, the love of Christ conquers all, and eagerness resides in the heart of the hopeful. Our citizenship is in heaven. And we eagerly await a Savior from there, the Lord Jesus Christ (Phil. 3:20).

> They sought God eagerly, and he was found by them. So the Lord gave them rest on every side. (2 Chr. 15:15)

20

A NEW WORLD IN SUBMISSION TO JESUS, THE KING OF KINGS

We look forward to a new heaven and earth, the home of righteousness. That's because the One seated on the throne says, "I am making everything new!"

With the kingdom of God within us (Luke 17:21), we sing a new song. Our trust is in Him. We live according to the Spirit's desires. We seek His will and set our minds on what He desires. He helps us in our weaknesses. In our prayers, He intercedes for us with groans words cannot express.

We serve God and those around us in the new way of the Spirit. We know that apart from Jesus we can do nothing. He is the vine and we are the branches.

We believe in the virgin birth of Mary and the death and resurrection of Jesus and the Spirit of God in us. We believe in miracles. We believe in Jesus.

We are friends of Jesus. We are children of God. We belong to Christ. God raised us up with Christ and seated us with Him in the heavenly realms. Streams of living water flow within us. He gives us life.

The kingdom of God is peace and joy in the Holy Spirit. (John 1:12; 7:38; 15:5; Rom. 7:6; 8:4–27; 15:3; Eph. 2:6; Rev. 21:5)

> He put a new song in my mouth, a hymn of praise to our God. Many will see and fear and put their trust in the Lord. (Psa. 40:3)

> Sing to the Lord a new song; sing to the Lord, all the earth. Sing to the Lord a new song, for he has done marvelous things; his right hand and his holy arm have worked salvation for him. (Psa. 98:1)

> Sing to the Lord a new song, his praise from the ends of the earth, you who go down to the sea, and all that is in it, you islands, and all who live in them. (Is. 42:10)

The Transformed Life in the Spirit of God

This is just a book. I am just a man—a broken one being healed and changed by God every day. The elders of my church family asked me to teach a class about "being led by the Spirit," and the trail down the rabbit hole, as Lewis Carroll said . . . began.

In some ways I feel like Alice when she says:

> "Oh, how I wish I could shut up like a telescope! I think I could, if only I knew how to begin." For, you see, so many out-of-the-way things had happened lately, that Alice had begun to think that very few things indeed were

really impossible. (*Alice in Wonderland*, ch. 1, "Down the Rabbit-Hole")

I believe in the impossible. I believe in miracles. I believe in the virgin birth and the resurrection of Jesus. I believe a person becomes a new creation in Christ Jesus through faith. I believe in the miraculous and changed nature that occurs in a believer through the Spirit's transformational power. I believe the gifts of the Spirit of God exist today. I experience them in my daily walk with Him.

Yet, even after all these years with Jesus, I now see that further growth exists in ways that seemed impossible a few weeks ago. These thoughts both scare and excite me because it means I must go down the rabbit hole. It means I must seek the Spirit of God in a deeper way, simply because I know this deeper place exists and He wants me there with Him.

Will you go with me? Though, now you may stop me and ask, "Where should we go? What will be required of us?"

We must go to a place where we don't yet know what is required of us. It may not be an easier place, but it will be the best place. It will be where all the action is on the front lines of the advancing kingdom of God. I don't know the way, but He does and if we knock at the door, He'll open it and lead us to a place where many need us. We won't get there by our own effort—He must lead us. Will you go with me?

To Go Deeper for Transformation

You, however, are controlled not by the sinful nature but by the Spirit, if the Spirit of God lives in you. And *if anyone does not have the Spirit of Christ, he does not belong to Christ.* And if the Spirit of him who raised Jesus from the dead is living in you, he who raised Christ from the dead will also give life to your mortal bodies through his Spirit, who lives in you . . .

For if you live according to the sinful nature, you will die; but if *by the Spirit you put to death the misdeeds of the body,* you will live, because *those who are led by the Spirit of God are sons of God.* (Rom. 8:9–14)

Did you receive the Spirit? Or, did you begin with Him, which all believers do, and then turn to living out your days in your own efforts? Have you been foolish in this way? Sometimes, after years as a believer, I forgot to turn to Him in prayer for the truth, strengthening, comfort or encouragement I needed. Instead I continued without His peace and with my own anxieties. Do you do this too?

Now, after this journey with you, I know He wants more of me, and I know something seems to be in my way. If I look closely, "It's me." Am I spiritually, mentally, or physically lazy? Am I too old? Maybe I'm scared of what is out there behind the door of His leading and in the unknown? Is it my lack of faith or my desire to keep holding onto the illusion that I control my life? Could it be because I feel others will disapprove? Is there a power or principality that doesn't want me to go? How about you? Where were you before the journey through this book and its questions? Where are you now? Did you knock at the door, or did you stop there long ago? Do you need help to grow further? I do.

The most powerful question Jesus asks us is, "What do you want?" Well, what is it? What do you want? What do you want Him to do for you?

Is He still breaking you of bad habits, or are the worst ones still within your nature and in control? Is He transforming your life? Is He leading you by His Spirit or have you been the same for several months or years? I can sense his movement and work in me. I pray you can as well.

Do you know that an amazing rebirth has occurred in you—that you were once broken and lost and now are found? Is the Spirit making you a new creation or are you holding onto your "sweet precious" (a ring or something else you need) like Gollum did even until his death? The Spirit of God is still working on me and I know He wants to do the same with you. Let us be courageous and not grieve Him. In Him is life. In Him, in submission to Him, are streams of living water. Pray, because on all occasions, this is true.

Miracles occur today. The Spirit of God brings the spirits of men and women back to life. He enters the bodies of believers in Christ Jesus. Does He dwell in you? Is He your everyday miracle? Jesus is in the Father. We're in Jesus. Jesus is in us (John 14:15–21). Today and tomorrow, let us look together for the evidence that He is in us and with us and guiding us into all truth (John 16:13). Let us look for a word from Him, for His words and for others needing His healing. Let us look for the living God in our lives.

The Spirit warns me not to make a fool of myself. Yet, without Him, without His guidance, I easily do. Do you remember Don Quixote, in the novel or play *Man of La Mancha*, as he battles windmills to receive his glory as a knight? He believes they were giants. He lives a part of his life within an idealistic prison of his own making. Sometimes he fights the wrong fights for the wrong things.

Whether for noble purposes or not, I've done the same. Have you? I pray we heed the warning and teach ourselves and our children the better way, the way of truth, the way of the Spirit. Then, He'll lead us to people like those Don Quixote tried to save himself—the Aldonzas of the world, "strumpets men use and forget," those who are mired in sin and who operate within the evil systems and behaviors of a world without God. He'll give us the words and behaviors to be His witnesses. As their faith saves them, they become the sons and daughters, the princes and princesses of the King. They begin to live a formerly "impossible dream" in a new kingdom of freedom—one that advances and tears down the strongholds of bondage. Their new life is free of condemnation and sin just as Mary Magdalene experienced from Jesus.

If we didn't know before, we do now. Though the Scriptures testify of Jesus, we don't possess eternal life by a diligent study of them. The Spirit gives us life when we love Jesus. Life exists in us because we have the love of God in our hearts.

When we love God and His Son, streams of living water flow within us, and we express our faith in love. We pray with people who don't know God, for their healing, for their encouragement or for their comfort. We help the physically, mentally or spiritually poor. We serve in the name of Jesus throughout the day. This includes our behaviors toward the checkout person at the grocery, our barber or hair stylist, our plumber or electrician, those at work and those at home—everyone. With the Spirit in us, we bring healing and love to the world around us.

Our houses are houses of prayer and the more we seek the Spirit, the more He leads us to pray. In this way, and in our behaviors, the people around us see us put God on the doorposts of our homes and businesses and the buildings where we gather.

Some of us find it easy to rebel or direct our own paths. Others stay unchanged, avoid being led and live a spiritually passive, empty life. Most of us want what we want and fight change. We all tend to do things in our own controlled effort, and when this does not work we look for guidance out of trouble.

Living by the Spirit and experiencing His leading and trans-formation require asking Jesus to give us victory over the war within us—to make clear our path and give us the power to walk it. It requires acting in faith and the guidance He gives us. We do not and cannot remain the same; and, in moving forward, open our eyes and heart to His leading. We seek His guidance in all our ways with all our hearts. We acknowledge Him and He directs our steps (Prov. 3:5–6).

We pray. We fast. We read and meditate on the words of God. We do His will and He leads wherever we go. We live this way to advance the kingdom of God within us and within those He brings us. We do this until we see Him in the new world where we'll be in His love forever. We do this for the King of kings, Jesus, because we love Him.

This Week

- Believe in miracles. Know that it takes more faith to believe in them. What if God chooses not to heal someone? Do you or I stop praying for miracles? No! We continue to believe and teach our children to continue to believe. We show others, through our prayers and steadfastness in trial, that God is real and sovereign and all powerful, and whether it is today or tomorrow He can heal anyone and bring them home.

- Look for *His leading and power and victory* over the stronghold and habitual sin areas set up in your body from past thoughts and actions. Grow in love, joy, peace, patience, kindness, goodness, faithfulness, gentleness and self-control. Shed your tendency to be judgmental and grow in grace.

- Live according to the Spirit (and not by your own effort). Allow the Spirit to control you. Serve in the new way of the Spirit. Live in accordance with the Spirit and set your minds on what the Spirit desires (Rom. 8:4–9).

- Take captive every thought and make it obedient to Christ Jesus. Stay away from empty deceit and philosophies driven from human tradition and the elemental spirits of the world. (2 Cor. 10:5; Col. 2:8) Meditate on the words of God and His Son and the Spirit. Allow the Spirit to make them a buttress and part of your armor against those things that dull the senses from seeing God's blessing, direction and power for your life.

- Eagerly seek the gifts of the Spirit, especially the gift of prophecy. Listen to and examine those who give advice regarding God's will for you or the church. Teach yourself and your children to test the advice with the word of God and with the thoughts of other Christians.

- Pray on all occasions especially for all the saints but also for anyone you see or care about. Cast your anxieties on Him. Go deeper in prayer, perhaps alone and in your quiet time with a language recognized only by God.

  And always, I pray, "May the God of hope fill you with all joy and peace as you trust in him, so that you may overflow with hope by the power of the Holy Spirit" (Rom. 15:13).

· · · ·

THE AWAKENING AND JOY OF A LIFE LIVED TO THE FULL . . .

*I*t's interesting that I picked up the uncompleted manuscript of this book two years after teaching a class with its material. I wanted to get it into final edited form. Each morning I moved from chapter to chapter until I arrived at the end. I thought I was finished.

Then I received this text from Denisa, my sister-in-law, whose prayer life in the Spirit is an example in this book. Here's what she sent me at 8:13 p.m. on Monday, February 13, 2023: "If you haven't heard yet, last Wednesday at Asbury seminary/university (a small community between our store and our home), chapel was held and has not stopped. 24/7 prayer and worship! I have been twice and words can't even describe what it feels like. A slice of heaven . . . people are flooding in from all over the country. So many people (over 2,000) last Saturday!) that they opened up a small chapel across the street. It is an experience of our Father and Jesus and the Holy Spirit all wrapped up in worship. Google 'Revival at Asbury' and read *Christianity Today*'s article. You are more than welcome to stay at the house when you come!"

Have you ever seen Steven Spielberg's movie *Close Encounters of the Third Kind*? In the movie, people find themselves drawn to an unfamiliar part of the world—not of themselves but of some mysterious force outside their control . . . for them something alien and not of this world. That's what I felt like when I received this text from Denisa. I turned to my wife, Sheila, and said, "I'm going to Asbury. I have to go."

On Wednesday, February 15, I entered the Hughes Memorial Auditorium while waiting just a short time outside on the steps of this historic 1890 building. Asbury College is located in the small town of Wilmore, Kentucky. About 8,000 people live there. There's only a Subway fast-food restaurant in the town and no places to stay. Lexington is 25 miles away.

My brother Mike, his wife, Denisa, and I entered the auditorium at the balcony level. A couple of students were leading singing with one guitar and a piano. The approximately 1,500 people below and in the balcony were singing praise songs to God. At times, with no piano or guitar, their voices carrying the music up into the air as they sat or stood to praise God. Amidst those singing, others sat in prayer.

The songs continued and it took me about 30 minutes to realize that this was not an organized spectacle. It was not a heavily produced performance. It was just quiet worship, the most peace-filled worship I'd ever experienced. I stood for four hours, occasionally sitting for short periods; and when I left, I felt like I'd been there 10 minutes.

Years before, when my picture of heaven was of hundreds of years filled with singing and worshiping God, I have to admit, it was not a thought that excited me. However, when I walked out of the auditorium something had changed in me. Today, a couple of weeks later, I still feel the same. I could go back and stay in that Spirit-filled worship forever. What I experienced was not of this world. Peace, humility, repentance, surrender to a loving God. A quiet wonder.

There was nothing in the town, college or the auditorium to attract the average person—nothing overly produced, no fine oration, no incredible lighting, no awesome display to tell others about. Yet, out in the sunlight as we emerged, hundreds and thousands of people had arrived from other countries and across the nation. They were waiting quietly in line to enter the old auditorium, even in the rain. It reminded me of Isaiah's prophecy about Jesus: "He had no beauty or majesty to attract us to him, nothing in his appearance that we should desire him. He was despised and rejected by men, a man of sorrows, and familiar with suffering. Like one from whom men hide their faces he was despised, and we esteemed him not." (Isa. 53:3)

I left that place changed and, after staying at my brother's home, drove back to Knoxville, Tennessee, on the Thursday, and then back to Asbury on the Friday. When I arrived, thousands of people were in a line that stretched out of my sight. I went into Estes Chapel, another of several chapels and places they had opened to stream in the worship. Inside Estes, as in Hughes, people were in peaceful worship and some coming forward to kneel for prayers.

There are many YouTube videos, blog posts and written material to tell you about the spread of this awakening into other colleges, Rupp Arena, and many churches and gatherings across the world. This awakening of His Spirit continues to spread as I write. The leadership at Asbury University, after Tucker Carlson reported on *Fox News* what was happening, asked him not to bring his cameras onto their campus. They wanted this spontaneous work of God to stay as it was in its humility and quiet reflection of repentance and hope.

You may wonder how to awaken, how to live life to the full, a life of peace and power, a life of freedom from bondage. If you do, as I did, then there's something you can do that will bring you this life. While not a life without pain, suffering or trouble, it will be a life of victory, joy and love—a life of transformation and of service for the benefit of others and the glory of God.

So, are you ready for the answer?

Ask God for His Spirit. Inquire of Him as you start your day and pray without ceasing. Do this with a heart of humility and love for Him. When you do this, life will not be easy, yet He'll come and you'll be blessed by His presence—with His power and comfort. Jesus died for you. Now die for Him.

Wake up, O sleeper, rise from the dead, and Christ will shine on you. (Eph. 5:14)

For this reason I kneel before the Father, from whom his whole family in heaven and on earth derives its name. I pray that out of his glorious riches he may strengthen you with power through his Spirit in your inner being, so that Christ may dwell in your hearts through faith. And I pray that you, being rooted and established in love, may have power, together with all the saints, to grasp how wide and long and high and deep is the love of Christ, and to know this love that surpasses knowledge—that you may be filled to the measure of all the fullness of God. Now to him who is able to do immeasurably more than all we ask or imagine, according to his power that is at work within us, to him be glory in the church and in Christ Jesus throughout all generations, for ever and ever! Amen. (Eph. 3:14–21)